IT'S BEING SO CHEERFUL ...

IT'S BEING SO CHEERFUL …

More Memories of Younger Days

Edited by Mary Davies

Illustrated by Fred Davis

The Erskine Press
2006

IT'S BEING SO CHEERFUL ...

First published in 2006 by
The Erskine Press, The White House, Eccles, Quidenham,
Norwich, Norfolk NR16 2PB

© Mary Davies and *The Anglian Pensioner*
Illustrations © Fred Davis
This edition © The Erskine Press

ISBN 1 85297 093 6

British Library Cataloguing-in-Publication Data
A catalogue record of this book is available
from the British Library

No part of this book may be reproduced in any form by
printing, photocopying or by any other means
without the express written consent of the publisher

Typeset by Waveney Typesetters, Wymondham, Norfolk
Printed in Great Britain by
Antony Rowe Ltd, Chippenham, Wiltshire

ACKNOWLEDGMENTS

We are again grateful to many people for the opportunity to publish a second volume of reminiscences.

Our warmest thanks for all those involved in the production of *It's Being So Cheerful...*, and in particular:

To *Awards For All* for providing the necessary grant;

To readers of *The Anglian Pensioner* who, over the years, sent us many accounts of pre-war and wartime living, from the nineteen twenties to the nineteen fifties;

To Fred Davis, our cartoonist, who provided pictures for the front and back covers and many other cartoons;

To our highly efficient typist, Beryl Harcourt, who brought order to the editor's chaos;

To The Erskine Press for valuable advice and unfailing good service;

To readers of this small volume in the hope that they will enjoy it and recommend it to others;

And lastly:

To the contributors whose reminiscences give those who came after some flavour of the times in which they lived.

Mary Davies
Chairman
ANGLIAN PENSIONER ASSOCIATION

PREFACE

This is our second book of mainly pre-war reminiscences provided by readers of *The Anglian Pensioner* who were children and young people in the 20s and 30s of the last century.

This volume follows *Can I Do You Now, Sir?*, which was a catchphrase (as is the title of this book) in the Tommy Handley series broadcast during the war – a little after the years principally covered here. We, nevertheless, thought the title appropriate for our second book, and both titles will be familiar to those who were alive in the early war years and, of course, to those living before.

The contributions were mainly compiled from entries to competitions held by *The Anglian Pensioner* newspaper, or items of interest submitted by readers or older people trained under Computer Training Schemes run by the newspaper some time ago.

Those who sent them in have, in general, managed to keep their interest in life and a sense of humour, in spite of the generally poor treatment financially of many pensioners by the fourth richest country in the world.

We are able to publish this second volume with the remainder of a grant received from *Awards For All*. Our intention is to send the majority of the copies published free to care Homes.

There will also be some copies available for sale and these can be obtained from our publishers. The Erskine Press, The White House, Eccles, Norwich, Norfolk NR16 2PB (01953 887277) at £4.00 a copy, including post.

Mary Davies
Chairman
ANGLIAN PENSIONER ASSOCIATION

"HOW CAN I PUT IT? TO PRESCRIBE VIAGRA IN YOUR CASE WOULD BE LIKE FITTING JET ENGINES TO A WRIGHT BROYHERS AIRCRAFT"

CONTENTS

1	Only One Careful Lady Owner	
	Jeanne Carswell	10
2	Tell Me the Old, Old Story *Arthur Utting*	12
3	Don't Go Down the Mine *Alex Coulter*	14
4	One of Fifteen *Peggy Moule*	17
5	I'm Not Stupid, you Know	21
6	A Funny Thing Happened…*Meg Ellis*	23
7	Rhondda Rendezvous *Mary Davies*	27
8	Solidarity Forever *Alice Cooper*	30
9	Well and Truly Drained *Doris M. Berloe*	32
10	A Suffolk Childhood *Christina Norman*	36
11	In the Valley of the Little Mill	
	Frederick James	38
12	The Way We Played *Beryl Harcourt*	42
13	My First Job *Win Francis*	44
14	Memories *Joan Fryett*	48
15	A Cricket Bat *George Miller*	50
16	Manners, Little Maid *Sylvia Colman*	53
17	My Sister *Mary Watson*	55
18	Times Were Such *Dennis Bidwell*	58
19	Four Legged Friends	61
20	Childhood Pleasures *Phyl Jones*	62
21	The Wages of Sin *Mary Davies*	67
22	Raised on the Black Stuff *Mary Davies*	71
23	A Tricky Business *Fred Jenkins*	75
24	A Parody of Sorts *Mary Davies*	77
25	The Poplar Councillors *Tom Stapleton*	78

26	Grandparents *Pat Wilson*	80
27	The Well Wisher *Mary Davies*	84
28	Our Lot *Alice Coare*	88
29	London Life *George Miller*	89
30	A Child's War *Lesley Sleight*	95
31	Life in a Boy's Home *Neil LeMaitre*	98
32	Any More Fares, Please *Fred Davis*	100
33	The Downfall of the Cabinet *Fred Davis*	101
34	Sense and Sensibility	104
35	A Hair-Raising Experience *Edith Pleasance*	106
36	The Surprise *Edith Pleasance*	109
37	My Big Mouth *Ivy Alexandre*	111
38	A Fisherman's Tale	116
39	Snippets From a Pre-War Childhood *Win Francis*	119
40	Wharf Street *Ivy Alexander*	121
41	London, North Eastern Railway	124
42	Old Age *Frank Hooley*	126

1
ONLY ONE CAREFUL LADY OWNER
Jeanne Carswell

I remember you then
An E-type among men
You pulled right away from the rest
It was just you and me
In your little MG
The others were really impressed
A dealer in cars
Trading in bars
Sales concluded over a beer
Your bodywork sleek
My suspension grew weak
Whenever I saw you appear

Then one sunny day
The fourteenth of May
We steered a straight path down the aisle
We drove off in your Roller
Drank rum laced with Cola
You really could do things in style

It wasn't too long
Before the kids came along
Boys, Morris, Austin and Ford
You viewed them with pride
But you couldn't hide
It was Mercedes our girl you adored.

The years wheeled on fast
And then at last
Your clutch was beginning to slip
Sometimes in the dark
Your plugs lost their spark
Your headlight on permanent dip
Although still alive
You'd lost all your drive
Your gear box a bit of a ruin
I know you'll agree
You'd have failed MOT
So I traded you in for a new'un.

2
TELL ME THE OLD, OLD STORY
Arthur Utting

Although now well over 70 years ago, I can still see that scene down at the Fish Wharf at Great Yarmouth in the 1920s. It was a common occurrence for my two brothers and I to wander along there and watch the unloading of the boats. The cranes carrying the baskets of fish would be swinging overhead as we made our way through the maze of containers which were being loaded.

Now and again a fish or two would slip off the basket as it swung overhead. These we would pick up and claim for ourselves, a practice seemingly accept on the wharf, for we did it often. Many a poor household in Yarmouth must have had a meal from these pickings which were made by their children. I often wondered if the crane drives quite deliberately caused the baskets to wobble and shed a fish or two. I remember well the shock we had when one morning we found ourselves barred from the part of the wharf by gates and fencing. It seemed that someone in authority had thought fit to stop our practice.

Were we so affecting their profits by taking the few fish we did? Or perhaps some moralist argument would be used to cover up the deed, suggesting that we were being corrupted by being allowed to pinch what wasn't ours. The poor just couldn't be allowed to think that they could take what they wanted. Such was the moralising humbug that apparently prevailed.

This happened about the same time as the events that followed, and they must have surely embedded a deep resentment of authority in my subconscious which I have carried throughout my life.

With my two older brothers and two other boys who lived near us, just off St Nicholas Road, Great Yarmouth, we often played on the stretch of beach between Britannia Pier and the Tower Building. It would have been around 1924 and on one of our usual strolls we saw a large Union Jack being raised on one of the refreshment kiosks. I don't know why, but I remember we all started singing a little ditty that I have recalled through the years.

Are you working? No are you?
Are you working? No are you?
Three cheers for the Red, White and Blue
Tell me the old, old story
Are you working? No are you?

3
DON'T GO DOWN THE MINE
Alex Coulter

As far as I can remember the summer of 1926 was warm and dry. We had just moved into my Uncle's house which belonged to the colliery at Hebburn-on-Tyne.

Houses were hard to come by and my parents were living in an apartment in Jarrow-on-Tyne, and my mam's brother had just lost his wife. She died leaving him with four young girls and three boys. We had two boys, me, Alex and baby Billy. So three adults and nine children lived in a house with upstairs three bedrooms and kitchen and scullery downstairs. There was a wash-house with a big copper for bath night.

Our school was a small brick building with one big hall, divided after assembly into four classrooms. Heating in the winter was by a big pot-bellied stove. Free coal was provided from the pits but there was no school meals or milk. In the winter a big pot on the stove was filled with water, liquorice and sliced lemon. When the mixture was ready we all lined up and the mistress would give us a dose to keep out the cold. Any boy or girl with a runny nose had to wait till the last.

Outside, at the pit, something was afoot. No miners had come up and the early shift was not going down. When we went home my uncle was there. They had refused to go down the mine as their wages were to be cut. The Miners Lodge had a meeting and all the miners were to hold a rally at South Shields in the market square. Next day, after their meeting, the Colliery Band and all the miners in their Sunday best clothes assembled at the pit head. All work was stopped, police surrounded the place. Our Head-mistress, who supported the miners, took all us children out of school and with our mams, grandparents and aunts we lined the street from the pit head. The banner took six miners to carry it, two on the main poles and four holding it firm with a line of rope. The Band struck up and off they went as proud and as steady as a Brigade of Guards. These miners had just come out of the Great war so they knew how to march.

Back to school and the day passed peacefully in our village. No noise from coal wagons, no dust from the pit head. Mam and her neighbours started to worry. It was 6.30 at night and there was no sign of the returning miners. 'Not to worry' she said, 'They will have found a working man's club or a pub and called in for a pint. By 7.30 all the children were in bed. In the distance came the sound of music, the beat of the big drum. 'Get up, boys and girls' mam calls. Outside men and women were milling around in one big crowd. Mam called out 'Gordie, where are you'. Other women called out to their sons and husbands. There was no order like this morning, just utter chaos

It seemed that the police had tried to close the miners' meeting in South Shields but the leaders had refused so the police moved in to remove them. All hell broke loose. The Chief of Police read the Riot Act and then gave the signal and police on horses with chains in between mowed down the miners. Police on foot arrested those lying on the ground and the meeting was over.

In 1926 the pit closed. Our life was in turmoil again and the whole country was at odds with their workers. It became the National Strike. Our teachers tried to explain what was happening but all my parents would say was 'Keep clear of the police and watch out for Lord Londonderry'. He owned the pit. Uncle Gordie said 'If you want coal son, go to the coal house. Don't go down the mine. Why? Let other fools dig it. Keep up top in the clean, clear air'.

4
ONE OF FIFTEEN
Peggy Moule

April 3rd 1924 I was born, delivered by Nurse Price in the flickering candlelight of a cottage home. I was the second youngest child of a family of fifteen children, ten boys and five girls. One of my earliest recollections was of my brother John, fourteen months older than me, who died of diphtheria when he was eight years old.

One cold morning I was eating my breakfast of a half share of a boiled egg with my younger sister, and three of my brothers were helping themselves to large thick slices of crispy fried bread from an enamel plate. It was still dark outside but the warmth radiating from the shiny black kitchen grate and the kettle hissing out grey puffs of steam mingled together with the appetising smell of cosiness. A gas lamp above the mantelpiece quietly purred and glowed, its pale yellow flame seesawed shadows across the ceiling and danced light over and around us.

My mother was pouring tea from a large brown china teapot when a loud knock rattled on our front door. Mother stopped pouring and went to answer it. Low muffled voices could be heard, then a wailing cry. We all stopped eating and waited. Mum slowly returned to the kitchen, her flower-printed cotton apron covering her face.

'Little John has died' she said.

'Little John has died' she sobbed.

John had come home a few days earlier out of the pouring rain, drenched to the skin, water oozing out of his boots after a day's caddying on the golf course. Within a short time, very ill, he was taken away during the night by ambulance to the local fever hospital. The same day the doctor came to our house and thrust long wooden sticks down the throats of both my sister and I.

'A swab' said the doctor.

Two white-coated men then came with masks over their faces and fumigated our bedrooms. They tightly shut and sealed up the door with sticky paper. No one was allowed in for two weeks, but the sulphur-like smell remained much longer. I was very frightened and bewildered by the whole episode but, as it turned out, neither my sister nor I caught diphtheria.

Diphtheria was rife in our town at that time, and an epidemic overshadowed our lives in the 1930s. Our mother was deeply upset when John died so suddenly and so young. It must have broken her heart for, two years later, aged fifty two, Mum herself died.

We lived mostly in the large kitchen of our eight room cottage. Around a well scrubbed wooden table ten of us could be seated at any one time for meals. The weekly bath usually took place in the stone floored scullery, but my sister and I were always bathed in front of the kitchen fire which hardly ever went out. Water was heated in a round brick copper, kept alight and hot by a raging wood-burning fire underneath.

Four of my brothers shared a bed in one bedroom and another four shared in another bedroom. During cold winter nights, two house bricks would be heated in the kitchen stove, then wrapped up tightly in thick brown paper and placed in the middle of each bed. Imagine the shouting and the struggle getting eight feet onto the warmest spot!

Clothes were often shared amongst my brothers and in times of real hardship, with wear and tear, often there were not enough boots or shoes to go around. Those boys without would miss school until another pair could be found. Most of the clothes my sisters wore were made by our mother. I remember lying in bed at night listening to the whirring melody of her sewing machine, and the joy next morning as my sisters tried on a new dress or skirt. Not quite so nice were the button up 'stays' she would make for us out of old horse blankets. They made us itch when we first began to wear them, but after several washes all the tiny chaff particles would disappear. We had to wear them throughout the winter months to keep our chests warm.

Equally I recall nightdresses once made for us. When mum ran out of material the sleeves were made of different cloth and of different colours. 'Your odd-fellow ones' mum would say.

Mother always made seven loaves of bread each day, and I usually had to hurry home from school at dinner-time and wheel the old family pram with loaves of puffed dough to the local bakery a short distance away.

The baker would place the bread tins, one by one, on a long flat wooden board and push them out of sight into a very hot oven. After school was over I would take back the pram to collect the loaves, clutching three pennies in my hand to pay for them. New bread, smelling like roasted nuts, and homemade plum jam was an everyday tea for all of us.

5
I'M NOT STUPID, YOU KNOW

Alleged to be comments from US Forces Evaluation reports

- Not the sharpest knife in the drawer
- Got into the gene pool while the life-guard wasn't watching
- Got a full six-pack but lacks the plastic thingy to hold it all together
- A room-temperature IQ
- A gross ignoramus – 144 times worse than an ordinary ignoramus
- A photographic memory but with the lens cap glued on
- A prime candidate for natural de-selection
- Bright as Alaska in December
- One-celled organisms out-score him in IQ tests
- Donated his body to science before he was done using it
- Fell out of the family tree
- Gates are down, the lights are flashing, but the train isn't coming
- Has two brains, one is lost and the other is out looking for it
- He's so dense, light bends around him
- If his brains were taxed, he'd get a rebate

- If he was any more stupid he'd have to be watered twice a week
- If you gave him a penny for his thoughts, you'd get change
- If you stand close enough to him, you can hear the ocean
- It's hard to believe that he beat a million other sperm
- One neutron short of a synapse
- Some drink from the fountain of knowledge, he only gargled
- Takes him an hour and a half to watch *60 Minutes*
- Was left on the *Tilt-A-Whirl* a bit too long as a baby
- Wheel is turning but the hamster's dead.

"HE WILL EAT THESE GENETICALLY ENGINEERED TOMATOES, DOCTOR"

6
A FUNNY THING HAPPENED....
Meg Ellis

Life gets complicated sometimes, don't it?

Funny things happen but, so that you'll understand this particular funny thing, I'll list the principal characters.

Meg – that's me.

Gracie – that's my sister who lives a couple of miles away.

Harry – that's Gracie's husband – not in the best of health

Fred – a Yorkshire friend of mine on a visit. He runs the local branch of Alcoholics Anonymous.

Bob – also a Yorkshireman. He's the local AA patrol man who sometimes calls in for a cup of tea.

Now Harry (Gracie's husband you'll remember) was in the habit of calling on me to pick up shopping, etc. on his way home.

Gracie worries about him and when he's late she gets quite agitated.

Gracie knows Bob the AA man but she's never met Fred (of Alcoholics Anonymous).

I was out.

The phone rings. Fred answers it.

Gracie: 'Is Meg there?'

Fred: 'No, she's out. She won't be long.'

Gracie (noting Fred's Yorkshire accent) 'You must be the AA man.'

Fred: 'Yes. That's right. I'm the AA man.' (He is very keen on his work and adds) 'Have you got a problem?'

Gracie: 'Well, it's Harry. He's not home yet.'

Fred: 'Is that unusual?'

Gracie: 'Well, he does sometimes call in at Meg's for a drink on his way home.' (She means a cup of tea)

Fred: (warming to his task) 'Oh' – (then tactfully) 'Is he…er… unwell, do you think?'

Gracie: 'He's far from well.'

Fred: 'Does he go to the AA?'

Gracie: 'Well, he's a member, of course. But it's some time since he had a breakdown.'

Fred: 'Oh, I hope he hasn't had another one.'

Gracie: 'I hope not. He's not strong you know.'

Fred: 'No, that's the trouble – they're not strong. We have to try to give them something to latch on to.'

Gracie: 'You mean like a tow or a lift?'

Fred: 'Yes, that's right. Give them a lift now and then.'

Gracie: 'I hope he hasn't had an accident…..do you think he might have had a breakdown?'

Fred: 'I don't know, I haven't seen him. Would you like me to go and look for him.'

Gracie: 'That's very kind of you.'

Fred: 'That's O.K. Perhaps he shouldn't be driving. I'll go and see if I can find him.'

He puts the phone down.

Enter Harry, dirt on his clothes, hands and face.

Harry: 'Blinking exhaust fell off and I had to get

under the car to fix it best I could. Where's Meg? I could do with a drink. Who are you anyway?'

Fred: 'I'm Fred – a friend of Meg's – on a visit. Are you alright? Your wife phoned. She's worried about you.'

Harry: 'Oh, she's always worried about me. Perhaps I'd better get off or I'll be in the doghouse.'

Fred: 'Do you think you should be driving......(tactfully) you look a bit done in....'

Harry: 'Well, who's going to see me. It's only a couple of miles from the White Horse to the Bear.'

Fred (alarmed): 'I don't really think you should drive. Come on. I'll drive you. I can walk back.'

Harry: 'What you talking about? I'm quite capable.'

Fred: 'Oh come on. It's won't take a minute. I'll enjoy a little outing.'

Harry: 'Oh well, if you want a run – but I'm not letting you drive my car....it's a bit temperamental.'

Fred (thinks): 'Well, that's one way of putting it, I suppose.'

They arrive at Gracie's five minutes later.

Gracie: 'Where've you been. Look at the state you're in. You had me really worried. Who's this with you?'

Fred: 'I'm Fred – you know, the AA man – the one you spoke to.'

Gracie: 'What happened to Bob then?'

Fred: 'Who's Bob?'

Harry: 'He's our AA man.'

Fred: 'What just for this village?'

Harry: 'No, not just for this village. He patrols up

and down – sometimes pops into Meg's for a drink – or the White Horse.'

Fred looks aghast. 'I'd better be going'

Harry: 'O.K. Thanks for the company. Mind how you go. If you want a drink, the Bear'll just about be open now.'

Fred leaves.

Gracie: 'What was all that about?'

Harry: 'I dunno. I told him I'd had to fix my exhaust on the way home and he insisted on coming with me.'

Gracie: 'Funny friends Meg picks up.'

Harry: 'I think he was a bit drunk, if you ask me.'

7
RHONDDA RENDEZVOUS
Mary Davis

A Welsh Bull named Llewellyn
Who weighed ten tons - or more
Thought he would court Sue Ellen
And set off with a roar
To take up his position
Outside her parlour door
              (… it was a milking parlour)

He watched the cowman gather
The chromium-plated tubes
And saw him place them carefully
Over Sue-Ellen's boobs
So - just as a precaution
He sucked a pack of Zubes
              (… so his breath didn't smell)

Llewellyn was excited
His knees felt rather weak
And very soon the dribble
Ran slowly down his cheek
As the beautiful Sue-Ellen
Her lover's eyes did seek
              (only coyly at first, mind)

Llewellyn flamed with passion
Till he could stand no more

And in a bovine frenzy
He leapt up from the floor
And with a snort and in one bound
He cleared the parlour door
          (it was only half a door really)

Now this caused consternation
Throughout each milking stall
And twenty cows all eager
To answer the mating-call
Forgot about the milking
And jumped the little wall
          (between them and the next cow)

Llewellyn in amazement
Just stopped dead in his tracks
While twenty cows, excited
Trampled each other's backs
And with their boobs still stuck with tubes
(I must report the facts)
          (it was not a pretty sight)

The cows were all a-tangle
They fell upon the floor
And stuck their legs up in the air
And meanwhile, with a roar
Llewellyn raised his mighty head
And bolted out the door
          (… well, I ask you, twenty of them)

Eighty hooves a-waving
Had kicked the buckets o'er
And all the milk, like ivory silk
Was spread across the floor
While love-sick sweet Sue Ellen
Was stricken to the core
                (… even cows have feelings)

She struggled in the slipp'ry mess
And - crying for her mate -
Bit through the tubes that held her boobs
Then, in an awful state
With hooves and udders flying
She rushed out to the gate
      (… she wasn't going to let him get away)

When passion had subsided
And they had quenched their fire
Sue Ellen walked with dignity
Back to the cattle byre
And Bold Llewellyn loped away
To join a Male Voice Choir
                (… well, he was Welsh wasn't he?)

8
SOLIDARITY FOREVER
Alice Cooper

'You Bert, Alice and Glads are to go to the Police Station with Mrs. Conklin' said my mother. Mrs Conklin was our lodger.

'The perlice station! We ain't done nuffink.'

'No, you ain't done nothin' but Mrs. Conklin wants you to go with Lally, Lennie and Freddie when she takes them to the police station.

'What they done then?'

'They ain't done nothin'. You go with Mrs. Conklin and she'll buy you some of those peppermint creams.'

'Can we all 'ave some then?' Bert asked Mrs. Conklin as we came out of the snuff-smelling sweet shop.

'Later on' she said. 'Later on.'

Arriving at the Police Station we, Coopers and Conklins, were sat in two rows on forms facing one another with Mrs. Conklin and the policeman standing in between.

'And what's your name' said the policeman to me.

'Alice' I began but was cut short with a peppermint cream while Mrs. Conklin nodded her head and said 'She's Alice'.

'And I'm Lally Conklin' piped up the youngest of the Conklin trio, seizing the opportunity for a peppermint cream.

The policeman turned to my brother Bert.

'And what's your name, young man?'

Bert had already sized up the situation.

'Albert' he said. He looked up at Mrs. Conklin

'He's my Albert' she said 'named after 'is father'.

'Yes, it's me Dad's name' said Albert, which was half true. The surname was a mere bagatelle where peppermint creams were concerned.

Gladys, who had fallen asleep, woke up with a start. She was missing something. 'I'm Gladys Cooper' she said. 'Can I 'ave a sweet?'

'Gladys Cooper?' said our interrogator.

Mrs. Conklin was quick off the mark. 'Gladys Cooper' she repeated. 'You know. The actress. Her dad always calls her that, doesn't he Glads'. She nodded, taking her peppermint cream from her mouth to see if it had got any smaller. 'Can I 'ave another one then?'

Mrs. Conklin obliged.

'So that's six children you have Mrs. Conklin' said the Policeman. 'They're surprisingly near in age.'

'Yes, 'e don't waste any time'.

The policeman nodded sagely.

'Ah well, sign this form and you'll get your National Assistance for you and the six children for the next six months'.

He winked at me – the eldest of the 'family' as we went out.

It was ten years later before I understood why.

9
WELL AND TRULY DRAINED!
Doris M. Berloe

My father was a strict man, and I often thought he would have been more suitable training a battalion of Royal Engineers from which he had not long been demobbed. The year was 1923, I was 3½ years old, my younger brother was getting towards one year old, and my elder sister, Frances, would have been ten. Dad had an enquiring mind and his idea of a pleasant Sunday afternoon was to meet Frances coming out of Sunday School, and take us all for a walk.

It often seemed a route march, to visit the pumping station of the local water works and watch the water being pumped into the reservoir; or maybe we might visit the sewerage works to see what made that tick over, or even perhaps the gas works to watch the steaming cooling towers. I was quite young but it was not a wasted part of my education.

On this particular Sunday the procedure was as usual. Dad in his best brown suit, well brushed and pressed by Mum who was wearing her straw hat which occasionally had the artificial flower changed to make it look different. My brother Len was dressed in some type of trouser suit and placed in the folding wooden pushchair which Dad kept in a well varnished condition. I was being got ready in a soft cream coloured open weave straw hat with a soft cream lining, bunches of forget-me-nots and rose buds at each side. Long blue and pink ribbons hung down from the hat in front of my right shoulder. My coat was made of cream Shantung silk, softly lined and the shoes were white canvas with an over instep strap and button, then I too was ready.

It was a long walk but I can remember enjoying it as Dad wanted to see the horses that the head mistress of the local school put into a field she rented. She used to buy up old and abandoned horses and put them out to grass for their retirement. Dad thought her very kind and was always interested to see how the horses progressed. We patted the friendly ones that came over to see us and then carried on to walk a different way home. In those days there was countryside all around us.

Mum was pushing the pushchair with Dad and sister Frances either side. We came to an unmade lane, just wheel ruts with a hedge one side and a grassy field on the other. We had only gone a little way along when, to my delight, I spotted a row of grass hills. Looking back, I think a lorry had dumped top soil, one load next to the other and they had grassed over.

'Please Dad' I said, 'may I run up and down those hills?'

'Alright' he said, 'but be careful.'

With the family walking beside, I was really enjoying myself. I suppose I was about on my fourth hill and running down the other side when I saw it. A metal drain cover, and the heavy cover was only half over the hole. In a split second I knew that my little legs wouldn't stop. As I reached the hole I tried to jump over it. I did clear the half uncovered bit and landed on the drain cover, and as it tipped up I shot down the drain and the lid turned over on top of the hole and me.

I can't remember being frightened. I was about six to eight feet down I guess. I stood there looking up at a very small chink of daylight. Then I could hear Mum and Dad saying 'Doris, where are you?'

'I'm down here' I called.

'Where?' 'Tell us where you are' they asked.

'I'm down here, down the drain' I replied.

As far as Mum and Dad were concerned one minute I was there, and the next- gone. Dad found the drain cover and pulled it off. Mum and Dad's faces looked a long way away. I could see them looking down.

'Is there any water there?' said Dad. I couldn't see but I scraped each foot and replied 'No, just sand and wires.'

'Well, stand still' said Dad 'and we'll try and get you out.'

In his lovely best suit he lay down on his stomach and held out his hand, but he couldn't reach me. He wore a 3" wide trouser belt with brass buckle. He took the belt off, went back on his stomach again and dropped the buckle down, telling me to get hold of it as soon as I could reach it, but I still couldn't reach it. I heard him tell Mum he was going head first down the drain and Mum was to hold his feet. When he had lowered himself a certain amount I could touch the buckle and told Dad I had got it. I wasn't crying and he said to me 'Will you be a good girl and do just as I tell you?'

'Yes Dad' I replied.

'Hold that buckle with both hands and when I pull, I want you to walk up the side of the drain. You won't let go, will you?'

'No Dad' I replied. I heard him tell Mum to pull his feet backwards, and I eventually emerged into daylight and Dad carefully replaced the drain cover.

Mum took one look at me, she seemed really cross and I thought she'd be pleased I'd got out.

'Look at the state of you' she screamed. 'Look at your clothes – you're filthy' and with that she gave me several slaps across the legs and then started crying. 'And look at your shirt and suit Joe. However will I get it clean?' By that time we'd walked across to the pushchair which my sister was holding and then she added 'Dad, get him out of there' pointing to my brother 'and carry him'. She then lifted me and sat me in the wooden slatted pushchair with such force that it hurt the back of my legs and bottom more than falling down the drain. Then, as an afterthought she said 'I'll know where that dreadful child is then'.

I was pushed home in disgrace. Even now I do not think I deserved the good hiding that I got for falling down the drain.

10
A SUFFOLK CHILDHOOD
Christina Norman

I was born and brought up in Lowestoft and my first recollection is seeing my mother weeping at the death of her mother. There was no money for a decent black coat or wreath, just a bunch of flowers from our small back garden instead. I must have been about five or six at the time. Then I remember, as if it were yesterday, the dreaded 'means test' man coming. He marched into the house like a lord, his eye fell on a sewing box which had belonged to Grandma. It had a lovely inlaid mother-of-pearl lid.

'Sell that!' he ordered. My mother was too upset to say a word but I remember kicking this awful man in the leg for upsetting my mother. He promptly gave me a clout across the head, glared at us, and left. The sewing box was later sold for the magnificent sum of 7/6d. I wonder what it would be worth to-day?

I remember my brother and I going to watch the Scottish fisher girls packing herrings into barrels and even to-day I marvel at the speed at which they worked. We would stand and watch as these lovely, kind girls threw us a few herrings and then they would enjoy the look on mother's face as she received this unexpected bounty.

I recall Bobby, a playmate whose family were even poorer than ours. He was always scantily clad and always hungry. Bobby used to come to school in plimsolls even in the depth of winter. As soon as he was old enough he joined the Army where he was fed and clothed. I can see him now marching down our back yard, so proud and pleased with his lot. Bobby was killed at Dunkirk aged 18, giving up his life for a country which had done so little for him.

11
IN THE VALLEY OF THE LITTLE MILL
Frederick James

The cottage where I was born was near the entrance to what was known as the Dingle. We moved into a house in the next village up the valley. Our furniture was moved by the local coal merchant who had a small Ford truck. My father was desperate for a fine day so that the furniture stayed dry as he, my uncle and the coal merchant loaded the open truck with the heavy Victorian furniture, together with an iron framed piano.

It was necessary to make two journeys and the most difficult part of the removal was having to up-end the piano in order to get it through the gate. They then had to turn at right angles, up thirteen steps to the bottom of the front garden, then up six more steps to the front door of the new house.

The house had three bedrooms upstairs and three rooms down, one of which served as a large kitchen. We had mains water but the tap was outside, as was the toilet.

The year was 1925. Downstairs was lit by gas when we moved in, but two years later a gang of workmen came to wire all the houses, giving us electric lights downstairs – complete with china and brass switches. We still used candles in the bedrooms though. Most of the cooking was done on a coal range, and in the winter we heated bricks in the oven, put them in flannelette bags and used them to warm the beds.

To eke out our household coal stock, my elder brother and I would go up into the hills to dig up tree stumps to burn. We also crossed the valley and the black river to pick coal off the slag heap at the Wylie Colliery. The river Sirhowy was known as the black river because of the coal dust which polluted its water and silt. Most of the land around us was part of the Tredegar Estate. Lord Tredegar lived in Tredegar House in Bassaleg which is now owned by the National Trust. For every ton of coal that passed over Tredegar land, Lord Tredegar received one farthing.

From the end of the branch railway line, goods were distributed by a horse-drawn four-wheeled dray. I think the horse, a Shire or maybe a Clydesdale, was the biggest in the district. Coal was delivered to miners' houses by cart. My father was a fireman at the mine and we were allowed one ton per month. The coal was usually tipped at people's back gates, access to which was by a dirt lane which separated the rows of terraced houses. Refuse was also collected by horse and cart. I used to jump on the back of the railway dray and have a ride down to the goods yard. One day I tried to get on the side of the cart and the horse moved and the rear wheel ran over my foot!

In 1930 I moved back to Cymfelinfach where a small water-mill was situated about two miles up the valley. I believe the English translation of Cymfelinfach is 'valley of the little mill.' I lived by the Workman's Hall, which was the forerunner of to-day's leisure centre. It was largely funded by the mine owners, but the miners paid a few pence per week towards the running costs. It was typical of many throughout South Wales. The basement consisted of a large hall which was used as a gymnasium, a dance hall and even a brass band rehearsal room. The ground floor had a reading room where most of the daily papers were opened and secured on sloping boards all round the room. There was a billiard hall with about three tables, billiards being a very popular game in those days. There were also meeting rooms. The top floor was a cinema and on Saturdays they showed Cowboy and Indian films, with stars like Buck Jones and Tom Mix. These were all silent films. I went by bus to Cwmcarn to see my first talking picture – *Tiptoe Through the Tulips.*

In those days it was quite safe for boys and girls to wander all over the place, and the hills above the village were our playground. In the summer our favourite place was up the Dingle, where we had a 'boys pond'. Every year, about Whitsun, the brook was dammed with stones and turf, the heavy work being done by young unemployed men. Some of these young men had gambling schools, a quiet place where they played cards for pennies or Woodbine cigarettes. Sometimes they were chased by the police and, if caught and convicted, could get seven days in prison. Many joined the Territorial Army as it relieved boredom and they had two weeks away in the summer camp. Many older men were also out of work and soup kitchens were set up where they could get a free bowl of soup and a slice of bread. Children of the unemployed were issued with free boots. The mine was called Nine Mile Point, being nine miles from Newport. It consisted of three pits, The Rock Vein, East Pit and West Pit.

In 1935 the mine owners were bringing in non-union workers from outside the district, so workers in the West Pit staged a stay-in strike. After a couple of days food was sent down to them. They stayed down for about seven days and the strike was believed to be the first of its kind in the country.

12
THE WAY WE PLAYED
Beryl Harcourt

It's a great shame that the children of to-day don't appear to have the opportunities we had as youngsters to make full use of the countryside. My brother and I had only to walk down the back lane and we were beside the river. Dad bought a piece of land there, which we called The Berth, and we spent hours swimming in the river, paddling around in our canoes, or sailing our dinghies. He bought an ex-Naval Pinnace which we used as a broads cruiser, spending our summer holidays exploring the many Norfolk rivers.

About half a mile from its berth was a stretch of river which offered a sandy beach and a very large, very dead tree on which we could climb. We called this area The Grove and held picnics there. A bit further on we could pitch our little one  man tents, almost opposite a dyke which led to the Postwick Sewage Works. This dyke had a very solid looking surface (ugh!) and it was also very smelly, but  we would paddle up it in our canoes and shoot at the rats which frequented it. Woe betide the paddler who caught a crab! We all had air guns and rats were a favourite target.

On my own for once I discovered a small inlet, the entrance hidden under overhanging branches, and paddling quietly into this inlet I found myself on a small lake. It was surrounded by trees growing from high banks, completely inaccessible except by water. The entrance was beside a large quay which had Connors Quay painted across the front. It has been suggested that this tall quay had been used to load bricks on to the cargo ships that came up from the coast and on to Norwich. The wood was rotten in places and the wording faded but it acted as a marker for the entrance to my secret lake where I would sit quietly in my canoe and watch the kingfishers diving in the water after the small fish they must have spied.

We carried on camping by the river, even after the authorities ruled that no camping was allowed within a 20 mile radius of the coast because by now there was a war on. We just camouflaged our tents and carried on camping. Dad had joined the Home Guard in 1940 and was put on river patrol so he knew we were there but he never let on. But all good things come to an end and as we gradually reached the age of conscription our numbers dwindled; first a couple into the RAF, then one into the Navy and I ended up in the ATS. Sadly it was time we all grew up – what a shame!

13
MY FIRST JOB
Win Francis

I was fourteen years old and had left school at the end of July 1939, with no real idea of what I wanted by way of a career. I had enjoyed my school days and was not particularly looking forward to 'the world of work', but Dad was a great believer in 'a fair days work for a fair days pay' so I had to get down to deciding what I wanted to do.

After some discussion, it was agreed that I try to enrol for a course that would equip me to work in a Children's Nursery. I duly wrote off to the Local Authority expressing my wishes, only to be informed that the current course had been ongoing for some weeks, and to apply for the start of the next one.

We were pretty hard up at the time – as we always were – so I had to look for something in the meantime to let me contribute to the family coffers. At a loose end, I went with Mum to town to do some shopping, and she being a loyal member of the Co-operative Movement and an active Guild Member, we went into the big central store. In the entrance, standing by the lift, Mum spotted an elderly, sallow faced man with a bushy grey moustache, wearing a grey overcoat and Homburg hat and black striped trousers. Grabbing my arm, she hissed 'That's Mr. John Bingham, Chairman of the Board of Directors – come on!' and she pulled me to where he was standing. At that moment the lift doors opened and Mum, with me in tow, followed the Chairman into the lift. 'I'm glad I've seen you, Mr. Bingham,' she said. 'This is my daughter, and she's looking for a job in an office. She's got a good reference from school and she's a quick learner. You know my record as a customer and a Guild member. She's my sixth child and I've never managed to get any of the older ones a job with the Co-op.'

Well, the poor man didn't stand a chance! The boardroom was on the top floor, as Mum well knew, and the lift was slow, so there was ample time to get her point across. She was a small but very determined lady! By the time we had reached his floor, Mum had extracted from Mr. Bingham a promise to 'do what he could for me' and he was as good as his word. Within the week I had a letter inviting me to an interview at the Co-op Security Check Office. I duly turned up at the soot- encrusted ancient building over a co-op store in the East End of Sheffield and with much trepidation climbed the worn stone steps up a cold winding staircase. At the top I entered a large open office with girls sitting round large square tables, probably 40 girls in all. In the near corner was a glass partitioned office and seated on a high stool at an even higher desk was a stern looking woman in a long brown overall with her hair in a tight bun at the nape of her neck. She motioned me into her office where she gave me the third degree and then the low down on what the job entailed.

This was the office where members' purchases were

calculated so that the amount of 'divvy' could be allocated every half year end. Each Monday morning the books would come in from all the branches showing the previous week's takings on carbon copies of the individual checks issued to customers, and our job was to add them up, and compare each day's purchases with the cash taken and entered onto a statement for the week. When all the branches had been checked, we then had to tear out all the first carbon copies, which were perforated, leaving a third copy in the book. These had then to be separated and sorted into every member's individual share number and tallied up month by month. At the half year end, the amounts were forwarded to central office where each customer's dividend was calculated. Pay out day was much looked forward to by all the hard up families in our neighbourhood, as it could be as much a half a crown in the pound – a real windfall for most housewives.

The young greenhorns like me had to do all the adding up in our head. The more senior and trustworthy girls had adding machines. One thing this job did for me was to improve my adding skills to the point where I can still tot up a list of figures accurately and swiftly. But I found the job wearisome and boring, and Miss Wilson, the manageress didn't make life any easier. She was of the old school – a real martinet who stalked round the tables to make sure we were getting on with our work. Many is the time 'Miss Tidy' would be yelled down the office if I was doing much talking – which I usually was.

Keen members of the Co-op would save all their checks for the half year and check their calculations with the amount of 'divvy' they drew and if they were in dispute we had to trail back through the carbon copies which we stored for about a year. This entailed three or four of us going into the storeroom where they were kept in numerical order. This was a musty room smelling strongly of mice, and on more than one occasion we found great holes in the paper piles where the mice had chewed it away to form a nest! I think the customer got the benefit of the doubt in these instances!

All in all it was a pretty soul destroying job and I wasn't sorry to be transferred to the office of our local grocery store, from which we dispensed milk checks, coal checks and threepence halfpenny club stamps. I was much happier there as I am sure Miss Wilson was to see the back of me. Unfortunately I never got around to re-applying for the Nursery Nurse course.

14
MEMORIES
Joan Fryett

A shilling a day on the trams.

A beautiful day out from the East End of London, near Epping Forest through to Key Wood, Hampton Court and Kew Gardens.

Sandwiches and pots of fresh fruit and jelly, with some brazil nuts as a treat, and a flask of tea or a bottle of lemonade.

Walking through Epping Forest in the autumn, the crunch of dried leaves beneath our feet, spotting fungi in their varying forms amongst the vegetation.

Helping my Dad on his allotment, taking the worms he dug up to the plot where he kept the chickens.

Wearing liberty bodices on top of vests which were hand knitted and combinations - an old fashioned leotard!

Brown leather gaiters smelling of polish, which we buttoned up from our ankles to just over our knees, using button hooks.

We wore panama hats in the summer and a white blouse over a cream pleated flannel skirt. In the winter we wore navy Melton coats and navy velour hats and leather gloves.

Our kitchen was always warm from the black, highly polished cooking range and smelled of an appetising meal our mother was preparing.

The scullery was warm on a Friday night when the

bath water was heated in the copper, a large round container in brick. The galvanised bath was hung on the outside wall when not in use.

Lighting was by gas and when you pulled down the chain it lit the gas mantle, a very delicate and easily broken affair, but it did produce a good light.

No such luxury as toilet paper in rolls – the daily paper was cut into neat squares and hung from a piece of string.

Ah! Those were the days.

"HE'S THE OLDEST INHABITANT. HE CAN REMEMBER WHEN WE HAD A BUS SERVICE"

15
A CRICKET BAT
George Miller

I recall the day father announced that he was going to make us a cricket bat. It was made from a plank of soft wood about ¾' thick. He lavished great care on it, finally sanding and varnishing it. During the manufacture he continually warned us about striking a hard ball with it. Its completion coincided with a visit of some relations. It was the weekend and it was decided that we would all go to Wandsworth Common to play cricket. As I carried the bat I claimed the right to bat first. I struck the ball and while awaiting its return my gaze focussed on a nearby drain cover. I suddenly had a distinct urge to dangle the bat through the grille. Had the bat been withdrawn and the game continued the incident would have been of no consequence. Unfortunately my skylarking act ended when the bat disappeared into the darkness of the drain. Most of those present thought it was hilarious, but father was furious. There was a price to be paid. Next morning, early, I was recruited to accompany him to the common equipped with string and bits of wire. After about half an hour of poking and probing the bat finally surfaced.

That was not the end of the bat saga. Despite being warned of the consequences of striking a hard ball, the occasion arose when a hard ball was the only one available. The bat ended its days in two pieces. While deliberating on some plausible explanations, the hand of God came to our rescue. The local curate happened to be passing and offered an excellent cricket bat that he had no further use for. I think we told father that we had done a swap. He thought we had got a good deal and we were out of trouble once again.

In 1929 I first attended Plough Road infants school. While I did not fully recognise it at the time I sensed that some form of behaviour pattern and pecking order was being established. One little fellow by the name of Alfie Day seemed to be the odd one out, continually falling foul of all concerned. One day mother gave me a large apple. On arrival at school I placed it on my desk. We all left the class room to attend assembly in the main hall. On my return the apple was gone. Raising my hand, it was quite clear what I had to say.

'Please Miss, Alfie Day has pinched my apple'. Before I could open my mouth, mistress said 'I have your apple. You can have it at lunchtime'. Suddenly I felt ashamed. Only moments before it seemed the most natural thing to do, then I realised it was a wretched act, condemning someone simply because it was expedient to do so. Later I felt relieved, firstly that I did not have the opportunity to say those words, and secondly that a quite an important lesson had been learned early on in my life.

Smoking, I recall, was among our 'verboten' activities. There was a vending machine that dispensed three cigarettes for a penny. We discovered that by pulling the drawer sharply it would partially open exposing one cigarette. With the aid of a razor blade you could cut through the thin wrapping and ease the cigarette out, manoeuvre the next one forward and carry out the same procedure. I suppose that could be classified as stealing, but not in the same category as mugging and there was a certain amount of ingenuity involved.

The past fifty years would represent a blink of an eyelid if they were related to the life span of our planet. But living in the mid thirties was in very stark contrast to today's environment. The Sunday school annual outing to Box Hill was like visiting a foreign country. On the occasion when a distant relative who possessed a motor car arranged to collect us one Sunday, we made sure that everyone was aware of the event. As we climbed in and drove off the neighbours came out to watch and we felt like royalty.

Today, expensive bicycles for all ages seems to be the norm. The fact that a full size British Made bicycle could be purchased for under three pounds did not appear to make it any more accessible to my contemporaries.

In March 1938, about six weeks before my fourteenth birthday, I walked out of Plough Road School for the last time. I can't remember the exact contents of my last school report but it ended with the words 'Should do well on taking up employment'. If marks were awarded for naïveté I would probably have scored TEN!

16
MANNERS, LITTLE MAID
Sylvia Colman

I was born in 1926 and lived in one of the newly developed outer suburbs of London. When I think back to those pre-war days it seems to me that everyday behaviour has changed out of all recognition. It would be hard for today's casual young to accept the formality we took as normal. Take people's names. Children never called grown-ups by their first names, but if they were close friends of your parents they would be called 'Auntie or 'Uncle'. Even older cousins were addressed like this. For some unknown reason names were a matter of great secrecy; we never knew our teachers' first names and it was a cause of great glee when one was somehow discovered.

Then there were ages. These were another source of adult mystery – sometimes children did not know their parents' ages even after they were grown up, and a child bold enough to enquire would be told 'I'm as old as my tongue and a little bit older than my teeth'.

There was seemingly no end to the ways in which adults ganged up in those days, presenting a united front so that they seemed like superior creatures from another world. I still recall the shock of realising as I grew up that they were really just as silly and fallible as children were.

You were always supposed to behave well at table, always asking to have things passed and never reaching across, but if you went out to tea etiquette was even stricter, and you were supposed to wait until things were offered to you and never help yourself. At one household to which I sometimes went the little girl's mother made particularly tasty buns and biscuits, and once, when several children were invited, there were two lovely biscuits left on a plate, one bigger than the other. Now, you were always supposed to take the smaller item when a plate was offered, but I wanted the larger one, so with diabolical cunning I offered the plate to another child. To my disgust she took the larger biscuit. 'What dreadfully bad manners!' I thought and, perforce, took the smaller one.

17
MY SISTER
Mary Watson

When I look back I wonder why I never resented her.

I can see her now, loping down the street, one foot in the kerb and one on the pavement. Her head is sunk onto her chest and she is muttering to herself. Every now and then she rubs her podgy little hands together in a quick movement. She does that when she is excited. The elastic in one knicker leg is broken and you can see her bloomers. The kids in the street call after her and I shout back at them.

I am fiercely protective of her – we all are in our family. I am nearest to her in age and she comes everywhere with me. She mucks up our games and when I have to look after next door's baby she rocks the pram furiously and I worry but the baby doesn't seem to mind.

Every morning I wash her and dress her and hook up what's left of the buttons on her boots. Sometimes I wind her hair up in rags and when I take them out it falls in ringlets. She likes that and looks at me with vacant blue eyes. She is my doll.

She sleeps in a little iron chair bed in the same room as me and wets the bed every night. It stinks but I just accept it as part of the pattern of our lives. After weeks of tantrums she has settled for three slices of bread and a ha'penny as the price for going to bed. She puts the ha'penny in a little enamel pot and rattles and bangs it outside the lodgers' door at the top of the stairs.

'Any money for the missionary pot' she shouts. Occasionally – very occasionally – she collects another ha'penny but mostly she only gets a muffled 'Goodnight Glads'. She never gives up. She won't go to bed without me and the ritual is as much part of my life as getting the sticks for the fire in the morning.

In bed we play games, like living in a house on fowl's legs or I pretend to be a monkey and she is my keeper. She takes me down to the shop and I steal sweets. I can hear her rubbing her hands in the dark. Sometimes we sing. She has a sweet true voice but some of the words are nonsense.

In the daytime we play mothers and fathers under the kitchen table and if the parlour is unlocked we take it in turns to play the piano. She thumps out tunes from the *Indian Love Lyrics* to *Yes we have no Bananas*. The melody is always true. Sometimes she sings as she plays.

I did resent her once. They brought her to our school to see if she could fit in with an ordinary education. She screamed and stamped and shouted for me. I had to go and stand with her in the hall the whole morning. She went home for dinner and didn't come back. I was greatly relieved. Apart from that I don't remember ever being embarrassed by her.

Why didn't I resent being lumbered with this ungainly, simple sibling? For one thing, she adored me and clung to me like a limpet when the world went ill for her. She posed no threat. She was my doll and my baby; my loving childhood companion. They sent her away to a home before I was self-conscious enough to be resentful or embarrassed by her.

    She is older than me.

18
TIMES WERE SUCH
Dennis Bidwell

Uncle Walt and Auntie Elsie's farmhouse was a square, sturdy building with slate roof and an impressive front door nobody used. A large pump was bolted to the side of the building connected to a well, but it needed a lot of persuasion to make it work properly. It was, in fact, a modern contraption in those days.

Although the farm was miles from anywhere it had once been a pub but who it could have served goodness knows. Knowing we were Chapel folk, Uncle Walt said the breweries were trying to keep up with the Methodists who put up a Chapel wherever there were sinners. Either way the house must have known a lot of happiness to make it such a pleasure to be in, with low ceilings, old oil lamps and a huge cellar that had a special musty smell.

Uncle Walt and Eric would turn their caps back to front, so they could rest their heads on the cow, squat on a tiny stool and start milking. Sometimes Auntie Elsie would help whilst our Mum and the girls made porridge and cooked the eggs that we boys had collected the day before from all over the farmyard.

Uncle used to sell greyhounds part-trained. He had a proper starting contraption which held six dogs and, when a lever was pulled, a bell rang and the front would fly up and out they would shoot. I had to pull the lever on a signal from Uncle Walt who used to pedal down the field on his bike towing a bundle of rabbit skins. The idea was that he should stay in front of the dogs, but it never worked. They used to have him off his bike in a flash. It was one big free-for-all. Nevertheless his efforts paid off because he bred a lot of winners and had dozens of trophies to prove it.

My cousin Ray was about the same age as me and some of our chores were shared, like getting the pony and trap ready. Catching the pony was the first task which was not easy. Her name was Kitty and she had been bought from some travellers for thirty shillings and a bike. We used to stretch a piece of rope between us and drive her into a corner, but the field was huge and our legs were short. Worst of all, Kitty thought we were playing with her. Eventually we would catch her and put our homemade halter over her head, but then we had to get her out of the field. Her companion, an old billy goat, did not want us to do this. He would butt you as soon as you got near the gate. The girls would not go near him.

The billy goat was kept as company for Kitty but to us boys he was like a mean security guard. We had to be very careful not to let him out as well as the pony. Quite by accident we discovered that if we made him cross enough he would stick his horns through the gaps in the five-barred gate, so you could then grab them from the other side and hold him firm. This made it possible to open the gate just wide enough to get Kitty out, but those horns took some holding so we used to take it in turns.

Recollections of happy childhood days like these stay fresh in the mind forever. Uncle Walt and Auntie Elsie gave a lot of kids a lot of happiness and what better epitaph than that?

"TROUBLE IS, I'M A ROTTEN GARDENER..."

19
FOUR LEGGED FRIENDS

I don't remember anything about the cars that passed our house when I was small. I remember the buses because I used them to go to school or occasionally to go into Norwich with my mother for serious shopping.

But I do remember the horses. The biggest horse pulled the Corona open cart which carried bottles and bottles of coloured drinks. The cart had large wheels with big tyres and the horse was so tall and his hooves large and smothered in long hair. He was very handsome. One day I saw him try to roll while he was still in the shafts. Must have had an itch on his back or something. He was soon upright again and no harm done.

The next one was a high stepping horse which pulled the dairy's two wheeled cart. He was very intelligent and stopped at each person's house without being told. The milkman had big churns on the cart and he would dip his measure in one, swish it around so that no one person got all the cream, then bring it to the door to fill our container. At Christmas the horse would turn for home, Dales Loke, and take his drunken master safely home. He always looked so energetic and happy to be pulling the cart.

The third one I remember was quite a small pony, maybe even a Shetland. She was called Queenie and we were told not to touch her because she was liable to bite. She pulled the greengrocer's flat cart which was so low to the ground that we could easily pinch apples from it if we wanted to.

20
CHILDHOOD PLEASURES
Phyl Jones

On reaching the age of seven I left the infants school where there were both boys and girls and went to a school for girls only. Once in school you sat at a desk and were not expected to move about. Discipline was strict and in our school, if we misbehaved, we were sent to the Headmistress and she would cane us on our hand. Our names were then entered into a punishment book which followed us through our school life and was a permanent disgrace.

School finished at four o'clock and we would race home. No mothers waited at the school gate and no cars were parked outside to take us home - it was quite safe to go on our own and we would hurry home for our tea. There were no school meals, everyone went home for a midday meal and because mothers didn't go out to work they had time to prepare it. After tea in the summer we would play outside in the road and with a rope stretching from one pavement to the other and held at each end by a boy or girl, we would skip as the rope was twirled and sing 'All in together, never mind the weather'. The child whose foot stopped the rope was made to change places with the twirler on the pavement.

When we tired of this game we would fetch out our hoops, wooden ones for the girls and steel ones for the boys. We would have races along the pavements and sometimes in the road. The boys had the advantage as they could steer their hoops with an iron girder while we girls had to hit ours with a wooden baton.

There was great excitement when the barrel organ man came down our road with his monkey perched on top of the organ. We would rush indoors to beg a ha'penny to put in the cap which the monkey held and sometimes we would be allowed to shake the monkey's hand. The old man played all the tunes we knew and we skipped and danced as we followed him down one road and up another.

During the summer when it was very hot, a water lorry came down the road spraying water from behind to lay the dust. We children thought it great fun to get as near to the spray as possible, often getting very wet as we followed it along.

The highlight of the summer was the Sunday School treat to the seaside. We went in a large charabanc, the seats stretching right across the body with a door at each end of every seat to enable us to get in and out. If you were small you had to be lifted in as the charabanc was very high. With the canvas hood rolled back we sat packed in together and we sang lustily as we journeyed along. On arrival we all made for the beach. Taking off our shoes and socks, the girls would tuck their dresses into their knickers and paddle. Our knickers were mostly navy blue with elastic round the legs and a pocket in the front for our hanky, not a bit like your pretty little panties of to-day. We would get very wet in the sea as we jumped over the waves and the journey home was very uncomfortable when dresses had been taken out and we sat with wet knickers next to our skin. I can still remember how horrible it was.

The winter had its pleasures too but so very different from to-day. We had no television to sit and goggle at but we had a magic lantern in our house and my Dad used to operate it and throw pictures onto a screen. We thought it was very wonderful and our friends used to come in and watch. We only had three different stories which we saw over and over again.

I often stood at the window and watched the lamp lighter cycle down our road and light the gas lamps. He would cycle along, stop, and with a long pole would reach up and pull down a little chain. The light would pop on and with his pole over his shoulder he would cycle on to the next one. Sometimes while waiting for him I would see the muffin man come along. He carried the muffins in a tray which was balanced on his head and he rang his bell and cried out 'Muffins!' in a loud voice so that people would come out of their houses to buy them.

We experienced the joys of a coal fire and sitting in front of it, toasting bread or buns on a toasting fork. When every house had coal fires in grates you can imagine the smoke belching out of all the chimneys up into the sky so instead of just a mist like you have to-day, there would be smog.

In the winter – especially in November – we experienced the 'pea-souper.' It was fog so thick that we could hardly see to walk a few steps. I guess we called it 'pea soup' because of its likeness to the soup which our mothers gave us, very thick and stodgy. We would be sent home from school very early in the afternoon and we found our way home by hanging on to fences or railings on the inside of the pavement. If you happened to be travelling on a bus in this kind of fog you took a very long time to get to your destination. The conductor would walk in front of the bus with a torch so that the driver didn't drive us into a ditch. This was very frightening.

On Saturdays, for my tea, I would have new crusty bread spread with beef dripping and I always used to dig to the bottom of the basin to get the brown jelly to go on top. Mum bought watercress from an old lady who came every week with her large basket and we ate it by dipping it in vinegar.

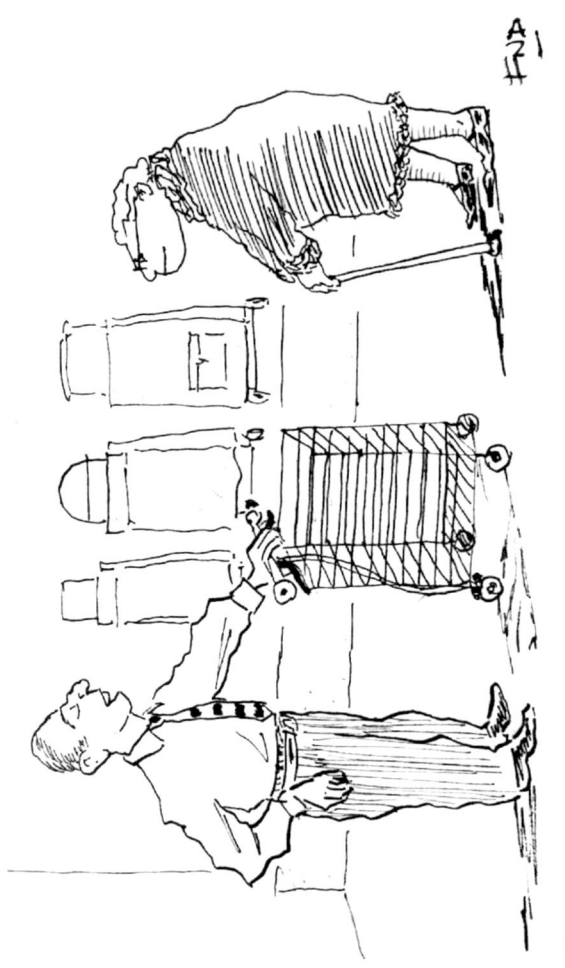

21
THE WAGES OF SIN
Mary Davies

'*Envy's a sharper spur than pay.*'

Lally Connor was prettier than me. That didn't bother me much until I was older, but half-way up her pert little nose she sported a pair of steel-framed National Health glasses – and that bothered me plenty.

Siddy Stevens, my boy friend, wore glasses too. The left hand lens was cracked from corner to corner. I envied him too, but only a little bit because he was the only boy who took any notice of me – and he let me try his glasses on now and again. We used to sit outside his house in the space where the railings were missing and he would wink at me with his one visible eye.

Enter now the villain of the piece, my best friend, Emma Lodge. She was a tall, gangly girl from the top class, a Monitor – and a Facilitator. She facilitated the stealing of dead flowers from the classrooms after school by opening the doors for me while I got them. She also once gave me some little brown pods to put in the teacher's coffee she was trusted with making. She was a girl I desperately needed to impress – match her macho, so to speak.

'I wear glasses you know,' I said to her one day after school.

She didn't seem particularly interested as she was full of how she had persuaded Harold Acton to wedge his leg under the desk, so he couldn't stand up to say

'Good Afternoon, Miss Bodger' at the end of school, and she had kept him in.

'I do wear glasses, Emma' I repeated.

'Where are they then?' she asked through a mouthful of bread pudding.

I evaded the question. 'I'll wear them tomorrow when you come round with the hot Milk for the Delicates' I said.

'You could, if you like, pour all the dregs into one mug and we could drink it at playtime' she said.

I didn't really like all that skin floating on the top but I said

'All right then'. My thoughts were on other matters, like how was I going to be wearing glasses when she came round with the Milk tray.

I spent a sleepless night and rushed up to Siddy's first thing to see if he would lend me his. His father, who was a policeman, met me at the door, so I told him it wasn't me who broke Mrs. Brock's window, and scarpered.

Lally Connor was my only hope. I bribed her with two pieces of everlasting toffee and a glass marble and she said I could borrow her glasses for the day so long as I didn't tell her mum.

I got all my sums wrong as I couldn't see a thing but I stuck it out until Emma turned up with the milk for the Delicates.

I beamed up at her through a dim haze but she was too intent on her task to notice, so I waylaid her after school and she walked home with me. The pavement seemed to come up and hit me but I picked my way along with one foot in the kerb and invited her to play for half an hour until her tea was ready.

We lived in terraced houses, separated by a crude iron fence with three uprights and two lateral bars.

Emma looked at this structure with a practised eye.
'We could do a somersault on that' she said.

She laid her lanky form across the top bar, tucked her legs under her, dived through the gap between the two bars and landed expertly in next door's gateway on her feet.

She did this three times while I waited in trepidation for Old Man Lyons to set his dog on us. Instead, I caught a glimpse of him peering through the curtains at Emma Lodge's knickers.

'You have a go' she said.

I pushed Lally's glasses up the bridge of my nose, felt for the top bar which seemed farther away than before – laid myself across it – and turned over.

It was perhaps unfortunate that the lower bar also seemed to have receded a few feet and I hit it with a nasty crack and landed on the ground, face down.

'You've broken your glasses' Emma said.

I peered at her. She was just a blur through my left eye and through my right she appeared in two diagonal halves, jagged at the inner edges. I removed the glasses. The right lens was cracked from corner to corner – just like Siddy's left one.

Emma decided at this juncture that her tea was ready and sloped off. I was left to face Lally, her mother, her two big brothers, my mother and Old Man Lyons and his dog, who had come out to watch the knicker show at closer range.

'You'll pay for this, my girl' Lally's mother said as I proffered the broken spectacles. She was talking to Lally, not me.

My mother tut-tutted and entered into complicated financial details about the transaction which neither Lally or I stayed to hear.

A week later Lally had her new glasses.

'You might as well keep those old things' she said.

I couldn't believe my luck. A pair of glasses, all my own, to swank to Emma Lodge any time I wished.

Who said crime doesn't pay?

What's more, Siddy and I could sit in the gap in the railings, gazing at each other with one good eye apiece.

'We woz meant for each other' he said.

With access to two pairs of glasses I had to agree we woz.

Well, at seven years old, one is apt to believe anything.

22
RAISED ON THE BLACK STUFF
Mary Davies

From his brimstone bed at break of day
A-walking the Devil is gone.
To visit his snug little farm, the earth
And see how his stock goes on.
                              S.T. Coleridge

Had he called at our home on his way back on a Friday night he would have found us mixing a bit of his mattress with two penn'orth of black treacle – a purifying mixture which might not have pleased him.

But for those of you who missed out in your youth on the elixir known as brimstone and treacle, let me introduce it to you now, and you too may grow up to be as clever as my grandfather who was brought up on the stuff. At the age of 87 he reminded us that he left school when he was nine and then added, with total conviction "And look how clever I am now".

My mother had much the same idea. On Friday nights I was sent across to the chemist for two penn'orth of flowers of sulphur. This looked like mustard with bits of rock in it and came, I understand, straight from Mount Etna.

It was mixed in a pudding bowl with black treacle so that the whole resembled a cross between slurry and partially-treated sewage. We were then lined up, all seven of us, and fed it – with a long spoon, of course.

As the spoon went down the line the viruses of the forerunners gathered momentum so it was not surprising that if one of us had chicken pox the others, after a suitable incubation period, followed suit in ascending order of virulence.

This, as it turned out, was not a bad thing. In those days, when one child in a family caught an infectious disease, the others had to be kept off school. Thus we were educated more in the breach than the observance.

One year my brother spent so much time in quarantine that he received the prize awarded to the child who had made the most progress. Being a somewhat spotty youth, the liberal dosings of brimstone and treacle he had received must bear some credit for this achievement.

To my knowledge, the black treacle itself was not an invention of the devil – but if it wasn't, it should have been. Some wag of the time added to Coleridge's verse.

> *He found a barrel of treacle*
> *With his brimstone bed to mix*
> *For he knew that all who ate it*
> *Had already crossed the Styx.*

It had other remarkable properties. Mixed with ipecacuanha wine, syrup of tolu (nothing to do with TNT though the effect was the same) and syrup of squills, it was a guaranteed cough cure.

Mary Basham, in her book *Look Back in Anglia* gives us another recipe – her grandmother's: '...add black treacle to paregoric, vinegar and laudanum (a penn'orth at a time).' You pays your money and you takes your choice. Your cough was either blasted away by the tolu mixture or the laudanum knocked you out till it went away. Neither recipe, it is hurriedly pointed out, is sanctioned by current medical practice, orthodox or alternative.

A time-honoured remedy for snake bite, it is not clear from my researches whether the black treacle was applied before the snake struck or afterwards, when the bite was sucked out. Probably the latter, which was bound to produce 'immediate expectoration' venom and all.

Black treacle was part of our daily diet – spread on bread when we had no condensed milk or stewed rhubarb. It was also stirred into Christmas puddings with a wooden spoon and a wish. (Mine was actually that I wouldn't be able to taste the stuff.)

How we envied those of our contemporaries who could afford the refined variety. It came in a pretty green tin with a picture of a lion couchant about to be stung to death by bees and bore the inscription 'Out of the strong came forth sweetness'. My mother insisted, however, that the unrefined sort must be stronger and sweeter. It was cheaper anyway. It had other uses.

My baby sister, having indented for a dolls pram one Christmas and having inadvertently been told the same day that black cats were lucky, poured a tin of the black stuff over our ginger tom. The cat disappeared for a week but came back restored to its original pristine marmalade and never needed a worm powder again.

My father, with an eye always to our cultural and moral education, sang this warning from *The Beggar's Opera*:

> *The fly that sips treacle is lost in the sweets*
> *So he that tastes woman, woman, woman*
> *He that tastes woman, ruin meets.*

I sensed, even in my tender years, that the devil was implicitly at work again here, but who would want to taste a woman covered in treacle?

But the real value of black treacle lay neither in medicine nor culture.

Mixed with soot, vinegar and water, it made boot polish. The tactile and flavourful properties of this compound were not lost on our same baby sister.

On the eve of the Sunday School outing, when our boots were put out to be polished, she pulled the tin of 'blacking' off the kitchen table and scoffed it.

True, there was no brimstone in it but my mother always said she had the devil in her.

23
A TRICKY BUSINESS
Fred Jenkins

The sign above the shop read 'Tricks and Jokes, Fancy Dress Hire. Everything for the Amateur Magician. Ken West, Proprietor.'

It had been a good run up to Christmas and now Ken was about to shut up shop after another good week. It had been a rather cold, wet day outside. Inside the shop was somewhat old-fashioned, even the floor was of bare boards and everything seemed to be in disarray. But Ken could put his finger on anything at a moment's notice.

The door opened and a man entered the shop. He wore a dark overcoat buttoned to the neck, a scarf wound around his neck and almost covered his face and his hat was pulled down over his eyes.

'Hello' said Ken. 'A nasty day out there. What can I do for you?'

'I want to see some tricks' replied the man gruffly.

'Anything in particular?' asked Ken

'Just any tricks' said the man.

Ken took several items from the shelves and laid them out on the counter. After saying nothing while Ken explained how they worked, the man glanced furtively around the shop.

'What's behind those curtains?' he asked.

'Oh, that's the Fancy Dress department' said Ken.

The man then walked to the door and turned the sign to 'Closed'.

'Why did you do that?' asked Ken. With that the man came back to the counter, put his hand in his coat pocket and pulled out a pistol. Pointing it at Ken he said, 'Now I am going to show you a trick. Put your hands up.'

'Oh come off it' said Ken and burst out laughing. 'That's an old one. You pull the trigger and a little flag comes down with the word 'Bang' on it. We sell lots of those.'

The man still persisted with the gun pointing at Ken.

'So you think this is a joke do you? I can assure you only bullets come out of this gun. Empty that till and anything you have in your pockets. Come on, and be quick about it.'

Ken went to the till and opened it. At that moment the figure of a man came through the curtains clad in a long dress. He said 'What do you think of this Ken?'

The man at the counter turned at the sound of the man's voice.

'Oh no! Not another tranny' he said. But Ken seized on that moment to dive behind the counter and pull on a short lever. The man disappeared through a trap door in the floor and into the cellar below. Ken came round the counter and, with the fellow in the dress, both peered down into the dark space. Ken called down

'How was that for a good trick? And by the way, this customer may be quite an arresting sight but when we get you out of there he will be arresting you. This man happens to be Police Constable Ben Roberts. He's been choosing a suitable fancy dress for the Police Ball on New Year's Night. I am sure that will be an arresting sight too.'

24
A PARODY OF SORTS
Mary Davies

To sleep or not to sleep. That's my dilemma
Whether 'tis easier on my addled brain
To halt the boomerangs of dull rejection
For a brief space; or sit down on my butt
And write a thousand missives, send them abroad
Speeding in all directions (but not yet forget
The s.a.e. that brings them winging back).
Or flee and have a kip? And in blest sleep
Relive the plots, the characters, the odes
That haunt my waking. That is an alternative
I'd heartily embrace. To kip: succumb:
To kip: perhaps to dream, ay, there's a thought:
To let in somnolence the visions come
When hands no longer ply the busy keys.
Romantic heroines for Mills and Boon:
A Tardis or a Tryffid, e'en a bare bodkin
To strike a bold blow in some nefarious crimes
I can submit in story to the Sunday Times.
Why should I labour, rack th'unwilling brain
When in sweet sleep the prizes are all mine?
The Booker, Whitbread, Toast of the Decade,
The Spanish villa bought, the mortgage paid?
If pigs had wings! Begone these thoughts of sloth,
I'll sit here till the Muse has had enough
I'll write a play about the kitchen sink
But first of all – I think I'll have a drink.

25
THE POPLAR COUNCILLORS
Tony Stapleton

I was born in 1920 in Chrisp Street, Poplar. My father had owned a horse and cart with which he delivered coal but, with increasing lorry traffic, work declined and he looked after a smoke house in Chrisp Street where they cured bacon in a large room with lines of smouldering sawdust and wood chips. Oak chips gave the best flavour.

I went to nearby Horton Street School and one morning the Headmaster came into our classroom and told us to 'Stand up and say Good Morning to Mr. George Lansbury' who then addressed us.

'Why is Mr. Lansbury so important?' I asked my mother.

'Lots of your mates' dads can't get work like your Dad so they have no wages coming in and have to get money from the Board of Guardians so their families won't starve. It's people like George Lansbury on the Council who make sure there's enough money to do this.'

I learnt later that, because Poplar borough was extremely poor, unemployment high and rate revenue low, George and other fellow councillors decided to withhold the 'precepts' payable to the London County Council in order to assist those with little or no income.

This brought George and his supporters in conflict

with the law and they were sent to prison. There they refused to work, demanded newspapers and addressed the daily crowds of supporters through the prison bars – much to the despair of the warders!

In the face of determined campaigning the government relented and, despite the anger of the Leader of the County Council, it was agreed to equalise the rates throughout the whole of the London area.

The stand made by the Poplar councillors brought the word 'poplarism' into the language of the labour movement. For me it was an early lesson in working class solidarity.

'He went to pieces towards the end'

26
GRANDPARENTS
Pat Wilson

My grandmother came from an old Norman family called Le Murl, but during the Napoleonic wars one of her ancestors was a naval officer under Nelson, and it wasn't a good idea to have a French name, so they changed it to Murley. One of my cousins was given this as her forename.

Emily Getrude Murley married John Whale sometime in the late 1870's. They had eight children who survived to maturity and lost several in infancy. There were six sons and two daughters. John Whale was a commercial traveller for Reckitts Blue, a commodity which was much in use in every household, so he didn't need to do much selling, so I don't think he worked very hard. However, when he was 40 at about the turn of the century, he decided he wasn't going to work any more. With eight children to feed and bring up it was necessary for my grandmother to do something.

She bought some material and made blouses and took them up to Bourne and Hollingsworth blouse department. The buyer liked them and gave her an order. One of the sons had just had St. Vitus Dance and to keep him occupied she had him turning the wheel of her old sewing machine. She was obviously a very clever business woman, because by the time the war broke out in 1914 she had a very busy factory employing about fifty women making blouses. Her children and their wives were all drawn into it. My father was sent to Singers to learn all about servicing sewing machines and my mother was a supervisor. Grandmother, by this time, had bought a large house in Brixton, South London, called Willows and an enormous bungalow by the river at Shepperton in Middlesex which had two kitchens, three bathrooms and five reception rooms with, in all, about 10 bedrooms. It meant that one or two of the sons could go to stay as well as my grandparents and all have separate apartments. It had wonderful grounds with acres of orchard, extensive lawns with laid out gardens and a long drive to the road. Despite the posh name – 'Las Palmas', the family always knew it as 'The Bungalow'.

One of my earliest memories is of a naval balloon coming down in the meadow and digging up the soil for ballast. Grandmother was furious, so in order to placate her the Officer in Charge offered her a small flight in the balloon basket. Neither my Grandmother nor my Mother would accept the offer but a neighbour took me, then aged about three. I can see it to this day, sitting on the edge of the basket, being held by the neighbour, Esme, and looking down on Mummy and Grandma who looked the size of ants.

Because he would not work Grandma kept Grandpa very short of money. But he did like his drop of whisky at the local where he would spend all his time during opening hours. He used to steal the eggs from the hen houses and sell them to the barmaid for his drink money. He would travel to the pub on an old tricycle. The drive was about three quarters of a mile long with two sets of gates to negotiate at the end. He would prevail upon my cousin or me to ride down on the bar at the back of the tricycle so that we could open the gates and he could ride through without getting off. We always considered this a great honour. My younger sister and her friends would hide in the ditch at the side of the drive, holding a string up high to knock his hat off. While he was dismounting to retrieve it they would run on ahead and do the same again.

During the war nearly all the work force were women. All the sons, except the eldest who was almost blind, were in the forces and all returned safely. One youngster, Roy, though didn't actually make into the war. He and his best friend Stanley volunteered for the Royal Flying Corps and were accepted. When Grandma found out she had Roy thrown out as he was only 16, so only Stanley went into the R.F.C. He married my Aunt who was the factory welfare person. One girl was found to be pregnant and when Aunt asked her 'Lizzie you must know who the father is'. Lizzie replied 'No Miss, 'e didn't take 'is 'at orf.'.

When I was five my grandmother was taken ill with sleeping sickness and was never able to walk again or take an active part in the business, but once she got over the worst and had begun to talk again, in spite of being in a wheelchair she directed the family on how to run the business. She spent all her summers at the bungalow and her winters at Willows. I spent much of my holidays with her and used to push her, or at least help with the wheelchair. She would tell me to deadhead the roses, which was almost a full time job, and some special roses she loved, she would eat the petals.

Grandma died when I was twelve years old, but I was twenty-one when Grandpa went. He looked exactly like King Edward VII and was very proud of his looks. He insisted on kissing my sister when she was small and she said 'Grandpa, I don't like your fevvers'. After Grandma died Willows was sold but the family kept the bungalow for a few years.

My Grandfather went to live with one of his daughters-in-law who was a widow with four sons to bring up, so was glad of the money the rest of the family paid her to keep the old man out of mischief. I didn't see much of him because when he wasn't trying my Aunt to the end of her tether, he stayed in bed! My mother said he was a lovable old rascal. The adults called him 'The Guvnor' and Grandma was known as 'Mater'. I think the daughters-in-law were all scared of her. Mother told me that the whole family had to go to dinner on a Sunday to Willows which meant about twenty of them sitting down at one enormous table. Grandma always carved the meat and served the puddings. When mother was engaged Grandma said 'Maud, which do you want?' Being very timid Mummy said 'I don't mind.'

'Don't mind, don't want, next please' was the retort, and so she got nothing. She was never that timid again!

27
THE WELL WISHER
Mary Davies

'The pump's gone' says Josh.

It's Sunday. The pump only ever 'goes' on Sunday – and only when I'm about to dish dinner.

This marvel of 1920s is a second-hand electric contraption we bought for £7 at Swaffham market. It seemed a good idea at the time. Four hundred half-turns a day on the old hand-pump and anything looked like a good idea at the time.

It is mounted on a little platform half-way down a 50ft well which never has more than 2 ft of water in it. The bottom of the pipe, through which the water rises intermittently, practically touches the well floor. Rotting pears, dead mice and the odd bed spring have been known to block it. The pump is just not strong enough to lift these things and the water as well.

Question? Do we eat first, with this sword of Damocles hanging over our Yorkshire pudding? Or do we leave dinner until after the well has been plumbed and the pipe unblocked, when the beef has turned to leather and the potatoes are ready to stoke up the wood burner?

We eat first. Unblocking the pipe is a hazardous operation and one – or more – of us may never eat again. We munch in silence, then leave the table to take up our time-honoured stations. We know our drill.

First, two tiles have to be removed from the outhouse roof so that the top part of the pipe has somewhere to go when it comes up for air.

Second, we each take a length of rope or strong wire, knot it round our waists, then tie it round Josh who is, so to speak, the man in the middle. Gran, being cautious, always chooses wire.

The boards are lifted off the well-top and Josh begins his descent. He spreadeagles himself like a horizontal Spiderman, bracing arms and legs against the sides of the well. Then all five of us – Mother (that's me), Gran and the three children begin to pay out lengths of rope and wire according to the muffled instructions coming up from the deep.

I look across to Gran. She has started a slow pirouette, having wound all the wire round her body and left none to pay out. We are insured for falling down wells, but being cut in half? Could they stick her together again? I make a mental note to tie her to one of the uprights in the outhouse next time – if there is a next time.

The children help her on her slow *danse macabre*. A length of pipe wavers unsteadily above the well top. This is the difficult bit. We all reach for it and try to guide it through the hole in the roof. As I shout 'Up a bit' someone else shouts 'Down a bit'. As I waggle the pipe to the right, I meet stiff opposition pulling it to the left. Another tile gets dislodged and falls, narrowly missing Gran's head which is now in the guillotine position. She is having her afternoon nap. Can they stitch back severed heads, I ask myself. Could I face a murder rap?

The dog has come to watch. He peers over the edge of the well and gives a loud bark. There is an answering shout from 20 ft. down which I hope the children won't understand.

The pipe is now up as far as it will go and is waving uncertainly at a low flying aircraft. I can see the pilot waving back. We steady the pipe with all hands while Josh examines its rear end. There is more muffled invective then a tug on the ropes. We begin to haul. With head still sunk on chest, Gran starts a slow pirouette in the opposite direction. I tuck her arms inside the wire to ward off internal injury.

Josh's cap appears – he rarely goes anywhere without it – then his face. It was not the face he was wearing when he went down. A few more heaves and he is on terra firma. Gran is still rotating so we wake her gently and everybody unties themselves. Josh replaces the roof tiles. The silence is deafening.

Eventually Josh reaches into his pocket and pulls out a twopence piece.

'How did this get down the well?' he asks icily. The children shake their heads. I know when they are telling the truth. Gran bends down and pats the dog and asks it if it would like a cup of tea.

We go back to the kitchen and switch on the pump. A trickle of murky water limps out of the tap. It has been a strenuous afternoon for Gran, who is not a well woman, so I help her up to bed. I pick up a magazine from the floor. It is open at a page headed 'Old Wives' Tale. I read: 'A coin thrown down a well for every member of your family will ensure good luck for your household for the coming year.'

There are six of us – and you can bet your sweet life she'll not have forgotten the dog!

28
OUR LOT
Alice Coare

My father plays the clarinet
My brother plays the drums
My mother hoots upon her flute
My sister – she just hums

My mother is all fingers
My brother is all thumbs
My father's hands are iron bands
My sister – she just hums – and she's clumsy

My mother smells like after-shave
My father smells like rum
My brother smells like plasticine
And stinks of bubble-gum
My sister – she just hums
    – and hums
    – and hums
    – and it's awful

29
LONDON LIFE
George Miller

The sound of the hand bell announced the muffin vendor with a tray of muffins balanced on his head.

'Scissors to grind, knives to grind!' was the call of the man with the tricycle, equipped with a pedal driven whet-stone.

The barrow dispensing pease pudding and faggots had it's queue of young and old clutching basins and various other receptacles.

'Stop me and buy one' was a household phrase and those words were displayed on the blue and white striped box tricycles operated by Walls Ice Cream.

The uninitiated would have difficulty deciphering from their cries what was on offer from the rag and bone man and especially the news vendor with the sound of his joined up 'StarNewsandStandard!'. The familiar air of 'Red Sails in the Sunset' drifted through open windows via the three valves in the magic box, powered by batteries and an acid accumulator.

These were the everyday street scenes in Battersea in the early thirties.

On Sundays the cry of 'Winkles all Fresh' opened many doors and a less frequent visitor was the shiny black man, bedecked in his feathered head dress. 'I gotta horse' was Prince Monolulu's way of informing the locals that he was prepared to reveal his racing tips in return for their hard earned coins.

A one-off sight was Britain's latest airship, the R101, the silver monster gliding gracefully over London on its maiden voyage. A few months later all that was left of the world's largest airship was a twisted mass of steel. Over five million cubic feet of hydrogen had exploded when the airship crashed on a French hillside.

The first useful act I performed, so I am told, was in 1924, lying in a cardboard crib and acting as a door stop at my Aunt Amy's wedding reception. No-one ever called her Amy, it was always 'Tiggle'. Her birth at the turn of the century coincided with a British was correspondent's report from the war zone in South Africa. He featured the river Tugela in his bulletins. Tugela became her nickname, eventually to be superseded by Tiggle.

Her husband Jack had only one hand. It did not seem unusual as far as we kids were concerned. He could have been born like it. They lived in two rooms in a three storey house in Shepherds Bush. Landlords used to let houses out to tenants who, in turn, sublet to others. Over the years Aunt and Uncle acquired the whole house, living there for the remainder of their lives. They did at one stage pay a £5 deposit on a brand new £300 house, but after lengthy deliberations decided not to continue with the venture.

There were a multitude of Aunts and Uncles but we were closest to those at Shepherds Bush. Later in life I discovered that Uncle had lost his hand in the great war. I often wanted to talk to him about the war but it never happened and he certainly never mentioned it. The nearest we came to discussing it was when I asked about a miniature coal scuttle. It was made from a brass shell case, about 3' in diameter. I think it was made in a German prisoner of war camp. It had pride of place on their mantle shelf at Shepherds Bush. From the way it shone it must have received the Bluebell treatment numerous times during those fifty five years.

After he died I learned that, at the beginning of the war, when he was only seventeen, he joined the Machine Gun Corps. He was discharged in August 1918 having been a prisoner of war in Germany. His certificate of discharge states 'No longer fit for war service due to right forearm amputated.'

I arrived on my brother's second birthday. He being only two years old I don't think I was the present he expected. We lived in a small flat in Harbut Road, Battersea. I believe that father was originally a plasterer. He served with the British Army in Belgium and was eventually invalided out due to mustard gas inhalation. He was advised not to return to plastering and obtained a job with W.H.Smith & Sons. He received the princely sum of £1 per week but the position did enable him to obtain membership of the Bookbinders Trade Union. The union card was a passport to better things – a permanent Saturday night job with the Sunday Observer. He received a payment of £2.3s.6d. This was an excellent remuneration in return for a simple task of stringing bundles of newspapers and removing them from an elevator. Due to

Trade Union influence a considerable amount of overmanning existed, resulting in frequent rest periods during the night.

Father married later in life than usual, having indulged in various sporting activities and an amateur stage act, singing Scottish songs. Some while after he married, mother cut up his kilt (I assume with his permission) to make dressing gowns for we boys and that seemed to signal the end of his past activities.

The age gap often has some bearing on the relationship between father and sons. In our case we seemed to be on different wave-lengths and a number of instances that we mischievously thought were hilarious, father did not think amusing.

Working on Saturday night, father slept during the afternoon. He drank very infrequently but always had a bottle of oatmeal stout at Saturday lunchtime. It was my task to fetch it from the off-licence. He always gave me nine pence and the empty bottle which had a returnable value of two pence. On one occasion when I was walking along juggling the bottle the inevitable happened. It slipped from my hand and, crashed to the ground. I expected it to smash into tiny pieces. I was surprised to find that it had broken cleanly in two, about three inches from the top. What to do? Take it back home and face father's wrath or brazen it out. Deciding on the latter I carefully placed the bottle on the counter. The proprietor unfortunately grasped the bottle at the top and it parted in his hand. His amazed look gradually turned into a big smile. The nice man rewarded my audacity by not insisting on the two pence (which I did not have). It may seem a minor incident but had father known I would have been on the receiving end of an harangue for my flippancy.

On another occasion, on Christmas Day, we were due to visit relations. I was sent on my normal errand to purchase cigarettes (20 Players Navy Cut 11½d.) at the little shop at the top of the road. As I was leaving the shop the owner said 'It's Christmas. Give these chocolates to your Mum'. I ran home and gleefully exclaimed 'Mum, the man in the shop sent you a box of chocolates'. After the initial excitement father said 'Where are my cigarettes?'. I furiously searched my pockets, realising that they had gone missing and, without waiting for instructions I rushed out. It was now raining. I arrived breathless at the top of the road. To my horror the ciggies had fallen on the tram line and a tram had passed over them, severing and scrunching them in the process. I trudged back home with the soggy remains. I was rewarded for my efforts with a whack round the ear and some verbal abuse that left me feeling that I was one of life's failures.

My Aunt Rose who lived at Notting Hill had been married to a German but he had died before we came on the scene. They had a bakers shop in the basement and substantial living accommodation on the first floor.

In the twenties people generally lived near their place of work. The bakers, the butchers and the general stores were a very important part of the local scene. Many of the customers bought their supplies on credit, referred to as 'tick'. The bakery was no exception. They lit the ovens on certain days in the year and locals would bring their meals to be cooked while they visited the local Pub. I think the charge was two pence. Soon after the war started in 1914, despite good local relationships, the angry anti-German mobs attacked the bakery, smashing windows and damaging the shop.

When father rented our first flat he apparently also purchased the contents which included two high backed armchairs and a chaise longue, all in matching green leather. When we moved to a larger flat mother wanted a more modern suite. The old suite had to be removed and father, in his usual forward planning way, decided that the chaise longue would go out of the kitchen window. He would remain upstairs with a rope, acting as anchor man. We boys were despatched to the yard (that was his first mistake) to monitor progress and take hold of it as it approached the ground. The first pair of castors attached to the thin legs were in contact with the wall; the line through the centre of gravity was not parallel with the base of the chaise longue. We would not have described it in that manner but we looked at each other and knew that as it progressed downwards the castors would run out of wall and crash through the glass fanlight. That is exactly what happened. An agitated ground floor tenant appeared and remonstrated with father who, due to it being wedged, could not pull it up or let it down. We decided that we could be of no further use and disappeared from the scene.

30
A CHILD'S WAR
Lesley Sleight

Towards the end of the Second World War my father was posted to Fersfield in Norfolk as a parachute instructor and we lived in what had been the Dower House of the local estate. It was the only house to rent in the area and it seemed enormous to a child. There was an antiquated central heating system but as the boiler took a hundredweight of coke at a time we only used it on Christmas Day.

There was a large garden with fruit trees and a wired enclosure for soft fruit as well as numerous old out-buildings for keeping chickens and usually a pig or two. One Christmas we reared a turkey, called Josephine, but when it came to Christmas dinner we were all in tears and couldn't eat her.

Rationing had very little effect on us and we were very fortunate at such a time of deprivation. Money was tight and my parents bicycled everywhere, including to dances in the Mess in full evening dress, often ending up in the ditch on the way home.

My grandfather was involved in the fishing industry and would regularly send parcels of fish on the overnight train from Grimsby. Only in the very hottest weather were they inedible, much to our disgust, but they usually arrived in excellent condition first thing the next morning. I can also remember him taking me to the docks in Grimsby to see the trawlers. He always wore shiny brown leather gaiters and one of my treasured possessions is his silver button hook.

My mother was famous for her dinner parties which usually consisted of a fish course, followed by rabbit casserole with force-meat balls and a pudding made with fruit from the garden or the contents of parcels sent by an uncle in Canada. A tin of ham yielded meat, fat for making pastry and jelly for soup.

I can still remember the delicious smells wafting up the stairs from the kitchen.

We always had joints of bacon which I seem to remember hung from a beam somewhere – probably in the vast cool cellar – and of course eggs, and there always seemed to be a group of servicemen sitting around the kitchen table eating bacon and eggs. My parents also befriended some of the Americans from the nearby airfield who were very young and homesick and loved to spend time in a family environment.

One would always bring me oranges and chocolate biscuits in a red tin with a swan on the lid and my mother would send them back to base with apples and figs from the garden. I was a very spoilt child at that time and no doubt missed all the attention when they left.

My mother had three brothers, one in each of the services, who also visited regularly and there were many attempts by my father and uncles to set up a press to make cider, none of which were successful, I seem to remember.

I can understand why some people look back on the

war as the best time of their lives as, although there was rationing and much deprivation, there was a wonderful spirit of sharing and comradeship and in many ways it was a wonderful time to be a child.

"I'M AFRAID MY WIFE SUFFERS FROM TIGHT SKIN. EVERY TIME SHE SITS DOWN HER MOUTH FLIES OPEN"

31
LIFE IN A BOYS' HOME
Neil LeMaitre

I was rather worried about the tunnel at Snow Hill Station. Big and black and round, but eventually our train went through without any mishaps.

In July 1939 I had been taken from London to a boys home in Moseley, Birmingham and now we were being evacuated to Somerset in early September. We went by train to Taunton, then on the branch line to Dunster, the last station before the terminus at Minehead.

Mrs. Louise Bowden's garage had brought two cars down for us. They were both big, open cars with a canvas roof. We all shouted to our driver 'Beat the other car!'

They had to make two trips because we were a large party – two nuns, a nurse and fifteen boys. The nuns were Sister Marian and Sister Susannah, members of S.I.E.S. (Society of the Incarnation of the Eternal Son – Church of England).

All fifteen of us went to the village school and eventually there were five classes from five year olds to fourteen year olds. Miss Pring taught the infants, Miss King the next class and when she smacked your hand she made sure she hurt you with her ring but, of course, you couldn't admit it.

The next class was Miss Hill's. I can't remember what she looked like but I'm sure she had more influence than anybody on how I grew up. Lack of room in the main school meant we had our lessons in an upstairs room of the chapel (now an art shop) on the corner of West Street and Georges Street.

We boys helped to supplement our rations with fruit picking – blackberries and whortleberries (remember this is the West County), wild rose hips for Vitamin C and gleaning. Corn was cut into sheaves and six sheaves were stacked into a stook to dry. Ears of wheat or barley could then be gleaned and used to feed the hens.

My eyesight wasn't very good (I am short sighted). Every year we went from school to the Memorial Hall to be tested. The person being tested stood in an open ended cubicle with the test card visible to those of us waiting. I learnt the letters off by heart. At least it deferred 'four eyes', 'Goofy', etc. for another year.

32
ANY MORE FARES, PLEASE?
Fred Davis

On this occasion in late summer 1940, the Luftwaffe had ignored us in the East End of London, concentrating instead on the City. I boarded the bus at Stepney Station as usual, en route for my office job (Junior Clerk – in reality – office boy).

We had no problem on the first half of the journey, sailing along merrily, but the traffic slowed as we approached the City. The reason soon became obvious – the offices on our route had taken a pasting and huge blocks of masonry, some as big as our bus, appeared as we slowly inched forward.

'Stonehenge' announced the conductor, deadpan, who was proving to be something of a wag. By this time some passengers had concluded that 'shanks's' was the best option and were hopping off the platform.

'Conductor, is this Algit East?' a woman shrilled from upstairs.

'No, lady' retorted the conductor. 'It's all git orf!'

33
THE DOWNFALL OF THE CABINET
Fred Davis

It was in the early Fifties, and Midge and I were living on the top, second floor of this house, divided, like the rest of the houses in the road, into 'flats' – rooms, in reality. Basements, ground floor, first and second floors.

I had been offered a kitchen cabinet by a colleague who had been lucky enough to be offered a newly built flat (a real flat!) in neighbouring Shoreditch, which we readily accepted. We were over the border in Hackney, ten minutes walk away through London Fields.

Now, a kitchen cabinet is essentially a large wooden box with drawers. It doesn't weigh a lot but is an awkward shape. I assembled my available manpower – my brother-in-law Phil, our mutual friend Chas, and myself, and we set out one fine autumn evening to collect our prize. After a little experimenting we decided that Phil and Chas would take the legs and I would take the top end. The thing was, I suppose, some eight feet long, about four feet wide and a couple of feet deep.

So, we set out through London Fields in the gathering gloom. We were making pretty good progress but, annoyingly, a large door on the upper side of the thing would not close, despite our best efforts to 'click' it shut and it emitted a dolorous 'boom' with every step of our journey. Just then, an elderly gentleman with his lady on his arm hove into view, obviously on their evening walk. He wore a black overcoat, white silk scarf and cap, and as he came abreast of us he doffed the cap, deadpan, and held it to his left breast.

We tore up our road at breakneck speed and deposited our burden in the passage. Then, after reporting back to Midge, I rejoined my companions and we set off for the local. It must have been about eleven when we let ourselves in to a sleeping household, dark except for a landing light at the top of the house, left on by Midge. Quietly we lifted our load and started our journey upstairs.

A word of description is now needed. The banisters in these houses start normally on the ground floor and proceed upwards. At the turn of the landing between first and second floors they are, to all intents and purposes, vertical, resuming a normal forty five degree angle once they have turned the corner.

We made good progress in the now sleeping household, moving silently to the first floor. And there we struck trouble. To manoeuvre an eight foot long rigid box through 180 degrees, at the same time making the thing stand practically upright required a great deal of muscle power from we three, plus the requirement to maintain absolute hush. Eventually we were round the corner and on the last lap to the second floor landing, watched now by Midge in her dressing gown, giving us a silent cheer.

I don't recall which of us it was who first noticed that the drawer in the cabinet was slowly sliding out.

At the head of the cabinet I reached out to halt the slide but, try as I might, my fingers were an inch away. Phil and Chas made valiant efforts to reach the drawer but, hampered as they were, could not quite make it. Despite our increasingly desperate efforts the drawer, so slowly but so deliberately, fell out of the cabinet and down, from top to bottom, two flights of stairs.

CRASH! BANG! WALLOP! Again and again until the damn thing came to rest below. The silence was shattered but no door opened below. Meanwhile we three were paralytic with – still silent – mirth.

The rest is anti-climax. We got the cabinet upstairs and we tiptoed down the stairs. I let my helpers out and retrieved the errant drawer.

There is a postscript to this story.

Next morning, Midge encountered Old Mother Butler who lived on the ground floor. She, Midge, put on a winning smile and said (in what I used to call her half-a-crown voice)

'Ai hope we didn't disturb you last night'

'Disturb?' retorted O.M.B. 'I thought the whole bleeding house was falling down!'

It just goes to show – there ain't no pleasing some people!

34
SENSE AND SENSIBILITY

'Now you're in a nice office job we'd better get you a sensible frock,' said my mother. Everything I wore had to be 'sensible'; shoes, coats, underclothes.

At least my stockings were not now sensible lisle – elevenpence-threefarthings had bought a pair of artificial silk stockings in taupe. Fully-fashioned, with a back seam flattering my legs, which I was coming to realise were 'whistle-worthy'. Suspenders, rubber with metal grips, dangled from the lower edge of my 'sensible' corset reinforced with whalebone stays which, at the earliest opportunity, I would fillet out, thus defeating the object of that restricting garment. To get back to my office frock, this was chosen from a mail order catalogue: bottle green in satin-backed marocain with self covered buttons on the long sleeves and at the neckline. The skirt was fashionably flared and to brighten its severity my mother crocheted a set of collar and cuffs in ecru. The material, marocain (my young sister insisted on pronouncing as 'macaroni') was just awful to wash: when wet it contracted into a corrugated stiff mass and had to be ironed damp then stretched to its original shape. I can't say how often it saw the washtub but I doubt it was weekly. But then, our underclothes were only washed once a week and no matter how much we scrubbed it was impossible to prevent the skirts of our petticoats from taking on a grubby grey shade. This was due to the frequency of smog and the general dirty air in London.

Occasionally my older sister, then around 23, who worked as a cook for a large Kensington household, would meet me from work and, after feeding the pigeons in Trafalgar Square we would go for tea and waffles in maple syrup at Lyons' Strand Corner House. There a small orchestra played light popular tunes and we would sit as near as possible to practice our flirting with the musicians.

On one of these days we agreed to wear our dresses with the sailor collars. Mine was actually one of my sister's cast-offs but we considered ourselves to be the cat's whiskers as, with a penny bag of corn each we attracted the pigeons. But wait … we were also attracting the attention of a distinguished-looking fellow with an expensive movie camera. We pretended indifference but he eventually approached and asked if we would mind him filming us. Did we mind? He told us he was a Canadian in London on a special news commission. We put all our talents into feeding those darned pigeons for several minutes and were then told that our 'performance' would be featured on the reel that had filmed the departure of King George VI and Queen Elizabeth on their coming tour of Canada. It would be shown in the cinemas of that country and, a new innovation, it would be in technicolour. He thanked us quite charmingly leaving us with an experience we still talk about.

35
A HAIR-RAISING EXPERIENCE
Edith Pleasance

Beauty, they say, is in the eye of the beholder. Well, the fellow who beheld that women looked more beautiful with curly or wavy hair did me no favours, nor I would think, the majority of my sex with naturally straight locks, although, he would have helped Teasy-Weasy and Vidal Sassoon to fame and fortune. As a child, when attending a party or special occasion, my mother would attack me with a pair of curling tongs which, when heated over the gas ring, would transform me from uninteresting to a Shirley Temple lookalike, albeit my hair was wont to bend rather than curl.

By my teens I was able to produce some sort of effect with strips of lead covered with a brown cotton material. These were my 'curlers', most uncomfortable when worn in bed. In 1938 I accompanied my father, a gents' hairdresser, to the Annual Hairdressing Exhibition at Earls Court. We watched in awe as the glamorous models were enhanced by styling, peroxiding, marcel waving and, wonder of the age, the new permanent wave – guaranteed to last! No more need for curling rags, tongs, pipe cleaners or crimpers ever again. This was the invention of the century. The answer to most ladies' problem! My father eventually acquired a second-hand permanent waving machine and instructed his lady assistant in its use. Julia, a rather cultured lady in her twenties, struck me as being for too superior for Pimlico Road with the smart West End salons just a mile or so away. The dingy back room, with its solitary iron-barred window at the rear of my father's shop, was surely no place for this ladies' hairdresser who, with her deep blue eyes seemed more like a sapphire in a paste setting.

Anyway, I was to be her 'guinea pig', although Julia preferred the word 'model'. So with feelings of trepidation and excitement I sat, ready to be transformed.

The machine resembled a netball post but, instead of a net hanging from the iron ring there were about a dozen or so metal hooks supporting dangled lengths of flex in untidy confusion. These leads terminated in bakelite tubes lined with coiled elements. Julia plugged the machine in to warm it up then applied a solution to my head that smelled like rotten eggs. Sections of my hair were then rolled in small rods and covered with tissue paper. Then came the exciting bit! Watching in the mirror I saw Julia wheel the contraption to line up with my head and, as though she were handling eggshells, tentatively fitted the sheathed sections of my hair into the terminals. A sound like bacon frying filled the room, followed by sparks, blue flashes and explosions in all directions. Each report caused Julia to squeal and jump back in alarm, making her way towards the door as though to leave me to it. My reaction was to follow her but, attached as I was, the infernal machine would have followed. When eventually it was clear that I had not been electrocuted, I was persuaded to suffer having the rest of my head cooked. I cannot remember how permanent my wave was but I don't think I braved that diabolical machine again. I was very relieved when, some years later, the invention of the machineless 'cold perm' came about.

36
THE SURPRISE
Edith Pleasance

I must have been around ten years old and my younger sister eight when we were told by our parents to '…expect a surprise when you come home from school today.' We weren't used to surprises, at least not the more pleasant type, so of course debated all the way home that day on what it could be. Another kitten (we already had three cats), maybe a puppy or, best of all, a gramophone, may be even another brother or sister. Yuck! The addition to our household that day, bought by my mother on the 'Never-never', proved to have a significant effect on our family and doubtless shaped the careers of me and my three sisters.

While other families on the poverty-stricken housing estate where we lived struggled to purchase such luxuries as wind-up gramophones, battery operated wireless sets and bicycles, my mother, who would use her pen to air her views on anything and everything, had seen fit to introduce a Remington Portable TYPEWRITER!

A brand new machine smelling of oil and printing ink, encased in a handsome black leather-like box, weighing in the region of twelve pounds. Solidly made, its keys were distinctively marked by white letters and figures on black background, each framed in a circle of bright metal – nothing plastic or even bakelite about this wonder. I very much doubt another family living among our depression hit neighbours owned a typewriter – the computer of the nineteen-thirties.

As mentioned, my mother wrote avidly so, with limited sight and being hard of hearing, the advent of this machine must have opened up a whole new world. It enabled her four daughters to teach themselves to type at a fair speed and standard and, very importantly, how to change the two-colour ribbon, clean the keys and maintain the machine.

Yes, I grew up with that Remington Portable, my mother's pride and joy, which became her constant companion and occasional fee earner for the next forty-odd years. I can picture it now and wager it is still in working order, despite the battering it received at the hands of we 'Learners'.

37
MY BIG MOUTH
Ivy Alexander

I learned from my mother that I could speak and sing from a very early age. She recalls that at the age of two I would sing 'Ain't she sweet. She's coming down the street. I ask you very 'conkidenkally,' ain't she sweet.' The spoken word was often a bit of a problem for me, and often caused trouble. As for my singing, the least said the better.

My speech was often followed by such coaching advice as 'Mind your mouth', 'Speak when you're spoken to', Don't talk while you are eating', Eat up and shut up', 'Don't talk to strangers', 'Children should be seen and not heard', 'Who do you think you're talking to, you cheeky cow?' and many other criticisms of my choice of words.

When I was about nine I went with my mother to the Chrisp Street market in Poplar. This was further afield than our local market in Rathbone Street, Canning Town but the longer journey – over the 'iron bridge' and a walk along East India Dock Road – was worth the effort. On this occasion the purpose was to go to the second-hand clothes stall. Each item was held up separately from a huge bundle and snatched up by eager hands. This involved waiting for some time for the right article to appear and there was much banter and coarse remarks among the crowd. A young man had obviously been trying to chance his luck with my mother, and noticing my presence remarked, 'Is that your child? You don't look old enough to have one that age.' I interfered, 'Oh, there are four more at home and some are older.' 'Oh, gawd' said my mother. 'They'd get you hung, wouldn't they'. When I asked why she would get 'hung' for having children, she said 'Shut up. You and your big mouth'.

I did wrong again later. I was about ten years old then. I can work out my age as I well remember my father's age at the time. He was never in paid employment but earned a useful supplement to money from the RO (Relief Office) by selling bootlaces, buttons and boxes of matches from a tray slung round his neck outside the Boleyn pub in Upton Park. Whilst he was out one day a strange gentleman paid us a visit. I opened the door. The following conversation took place.

'Is your father in?'

'No' I said.

'Where is he?'

'Out working'

'How old is he?'

'47' I replied

When my father returned I told him of the visit. I thought I had been so clever as I answered all the questions right. I even knew his age.

'You stupid bastard' my father said and whacked me across the mouth. My mother did give me an explanation for this.

'The man was probably from the RO' she said. 'You and your big mouth.'

Even at school I opened my mouth inappropriately. I was in the final class at the Bidder Street Junior Mixed School. It was my second year there, as I had skipped a year. I was bored and impatient and 'knew all the answers'. I was constantly told by my teacher, 'Dolly' Dowling, to keep quiet, and to help me to do this I was given a long length of Hessian to embroider. I could do what I liked with it, and I did. It was kept in a large wicker-work basket which was secured with a padlock. One day the key was missing so I could not gain access to my masterpiece. I must have driven poor Dolly to distraction as she sent for the caretaker to unlock the basket. This he did in no time. Satisfied, I put my hands on my hips and said 'At last. It just shows what some men can do, doesn't it'. They looked at each other quizzically, and I heard Dolly say, 'She's heard that expression somewhere'. I gathered I should have just said 'thank you'. At least I did not get a smack in my big mouth. This followed shortly afterwards at home.

My father, who had been a professional boxer, was not always easy to understand. His speech was muffled and slurred, 'Due to boxing, you know'. He also had a lurid vocabulary, generally associated with 'troopers'. On one occasion when I didn't understand him, I said 'What?'. I learned later that I should have said 'I beg your pardon'. He was furious. 'Don't 'what' me, you ignorant bastard. Learn to speak properly' he said and followed this expletive with the now obligatory smack in the mouth. Oops! 'Watch your mouth' said my mother, or did she say 'Wash your mouth'?

A few weeks later I passed the scholarship and went to the Russell Central School in Queens Road, Upton Park, and I did learn to speak properly. Part of the curriculum included elocution lessons, given by the po-faced Miss Male. We thought these were hilarious. At least I learned to articulate clearly. My problem seemed to be 'putting my foot in it' too often when I opened my mouth.

It was during my first Domestic Science lesson that I made my next gaff. We had instructions on how to lay a table and to get all the place settings in some sort of order. The place mat was surrounded by implements. Some knives had curly edges. These were called fish knives. Fish knives? I thought fish was eaten out of newspapers. Apparently, to tackle this array of cutlery, one started from the outside and worked inwards. 'And what else should we do?' asked Miss Marchant. Hands shot up offering suggestions until no more were forthcoming. I thought I'd be clever and wracked my brains. A few years previously I had been the recipient of free school meals, which I found nauseous, but unless we had cleared the plate we were not allowed any 'afters'. However, in order to survive I had to eat, so to clear my plate I would throw the left over food under the table, and most of my dining companions did likewise. We were then rewarded with rice, or sago pudding. We knew we shouldn't do this but we could not allow ourselves to go hungry. 'Right Miss Marchant,' I thought, 'I know one' and my hand shot up. 'Please Miss, if you don't like the food, don't throw it under the table.' I could tell by the response I had said the wrong thing again. But I was now on a learning curve. I could articulate and say 'I beg your pardon' but I now had to think before I spoke. I still spoke too much though. On my first school report the form teacher had written 'Works well but is rather talkative in class.'

Knowing when to speak and when not to speak still baffles me, but I don't worry so much now. I take the view that, when in doubt, speak up. At least I can do this now without getting a smack in the mouth. The turning point came when I was seventeen, during the war and I was the only one of six children to remain at home with my mother and father. One brother was in the army and another in hospital. My sister was in the WAAFs and a younger brother and sister were evacuated. It was evening time and my mother had prepared a packed lunch for my father to take with him when he went on ARP duty. He took a dislike to the contents and threw everything at her, box as well. I spoke up 'Don't you treat my mother like that'.

Wow! All hell was let loose. I had a black eye as well as a smack in the mouth. I'm delighted to say that was the last smack in the mouth I received for speaking out of turn. After he left, I said to my mother.

'I'm leaving home. You can stay if you like, but I'm going.' In the event she left too. A few days later we found an empty, slightly bomb-damaged flat, and moved in. Me and my big mouth.

38
A FISHERMAN'S TALE

I started work at Dunbars as a herring curer. Me and my brother Angus (Innis) went to Aberdeen with my father, nick-named Wee Butt, as my brother was going to join the Gordon Highlanders and I was going to join the Royal Navy. My brother passed his examination to join up but I failed mine as I had adenoids which affected my swimming.

It was 1938 and I decided to start work on a fishing boat and joined the *Primrose ER233* as cook. My skipper, who we called Willie, was a good teacher and what I would call a gentleman. I got to know the crew and two of them became my best pals. Their names were David Stracham who played the trumpet in the Presley Dance Band, and David Duthie.

I learnt a lot about the sea. We went out every night setting the herring nets. These hang like curtains in the sea. There are floats on top of the nets which are full of air and also corks, and a tarry leader at the bottom as an anchor to keep the nets straight. The leader was about three miles long. Once the nets were set we had time for a few hours sleep while one of the fishermen kept his eyes on the floats. We were woken when it was time to haul in the nets. My job when we were recovering the nets was to coil the leader into a box underneath the capstan. It was a wet job as the leader was still dripping from the sea.

Willie Ross, another crew member, taught me how to use the compass. I also learnt how to take the *Primrose* into harbour. After I had cooked the crew's breakfast and while they ate, I was at the steering wheel and learned to recognise the Broch motor boats and drifters, named after the drift-net fishing they did.

When the fishing season finished I was paid my wages which I took home to my mother. This was more than my father was earning. I was asked by the skipper, Willie, if I would like to go to Lowestoft. I said 'Yes' but would have to ask my mother. Both mum and dad said I could go. By now I was on regular wages plus my work on deck and scram money.

On our voyage down to Lowestoft the crew showed me how to cook and helped me pass the time even cleaning and painting and dubbing their clothes. As we were racing down at about eight knots by our log we used our mizzen sail which increased our speed. As the crew had their women folk down in Lowestoft a lot of their chests of clothes had been put on our boat and stowed away for them.

We had a successful year at the Lowestoft fishing with plenty of crans of herring but then had to return home and I remember, as we were coming down on the trip, I heard our Skipper say 'We are due for bad weather' and as we were on passage to put into North Shields Fisherman's Wharf I said to the Skipper 'Can I have two and sixpence out of my wages?' He asked me why I wanted the money. I told him I wanted to go to the cinema but he told me 'We are on a barter system.

You don't need money. Wash a couple of jam jars and I will take you up there.'

I had my tea, washed up, and was ready to go. Off we went to the Wooden Dolly picture house. He explained to me there was a Wooden Dolly with her fish creel on her back as everything was to do with fishing in the Shields, and the Wooden Dolly is still there today. I entered the cinema, as he had told me to do, approached the pay box and gave the jars to the ticket lady. She gave me two tickets, one for the cinema and one for a bar of chocolate. The skipper left me there and returned to the boat.

The show was a silent movie called All Quiet on the Western Front from World War One, which I enjoyed. I returned to the *Primrose*, fell asleep and we were at sea when I awoke to do the crews' breakfast. I had to tell them all about the film and the antics Charlie Chaplin had got up to. I will always remember the songs and his baggy trousers.

On our arrival home our skipper went ashore to the fishing broker to draw wages for the crew. I received £82 for my work. I took the money with my clothes and donkey breakfast and blankets with a promise to keep in touch. It was now winter with us.

I gave my mother the money I had been paid and she cried. She told me she had never seen so much money in all her life. 'Come down the street' she said. 'We will get you a new suit, laddie.' She picked me a nice double-breasted suit, brown in colour. I did feel like a Toff!

39
SNIPPETS FROM A PRE-WAR CHILDHOOD
Win Francis

As a girl next to the youngest of seven children in the 1920s life was pretty hard. Dad was a coremaker in a foundry and although this was a skilled job he didn't get a big wage. On top of that he had a weak chest, probably exacerbated by the dust and grit of the foundry, and he was often off work in the winter with bronchitis.

My three older sisters went into service soon after leaving school, two in Matlock and one at Southport. I don't know how we all fitted into our small three-bedroom terraced house. I was too young at the time to be aware of it but I've since thought that that lack of space, as well as scarcity of jobs, was one of the reasons why so many young lads went into the forces and girls into service.

My mother, like a lot of her contemporaries, took in washing to help with the family finances. One of her customers was the local butcher's wife, Mrs Mirfin, who had a daughter in my class at school. My youngest sister, Kathleen, was the lucky recipient of some lovely hand-me-downs from her. I still remember two dresses in particular – one dark green velvet and one a natural shantung with frills from the waist, each one embroidered with a butterfly. I was very envious as they were expensive dresses and I would have loved to show off in them. Mum made many of our frocks and, though the fabric was good and usually pretty, the styling was very 'everyday wear'.

My older brother Jack was working for a firm delivering milk to shops, and I well remember on occasions being sent after school on pay-day to pick up his wages from him so mum could buy something for Friday tea before dad got home from work.

Times were hard, but it was the same for all the families in our neighbourhood, so we didn't feel particularly deprived and we kids enjoyed our childhood and the closeness of family and friends.

From Fred Davies; our Attleborough cartoonist

"HELLO, MR. JONES. YOUNG SMITHERS HERE WILL BE DOING YOUR OPERATION - HE NEEDS THE WORK EXPERIENCE"

40
WHARF STREET
Ivy Alexander

I was delighted to receive six typed A4 pages from a 93 year old former Customs Officer from Harwich. He worked in the London docks from 1932 to 1938 and came to know East Ham when he was posted to the Albert Dock.

He writes: 'You would have shared my horror at seeing a fleet of dustcarts proceeding through West Ham loaded with perfectly good bananas bound for destruction because they were ripe, and passing so much poverty where they would have been good and tasteful nourishment. Even worse, any ripe fruit was deposited in bond at the quayside for outside collection and dockers were actually prosecuted for helping themselves.'

However, where the dockers waited hopefully 'on the stones' to be selected for low-paid and often unpleasant

work is now transformed. They would not recognise the Victoria docks or indeed any of the docks where they once worked. Many, like St Katherine's Dock, are now tourist attractions.

Growing up in West Ham I had assumed it would last forever and that we were 'all of a kind'. I now realise that West Ham was created by people from a variety of backgrounds. There were displaced illiterate farm labourers, immigrants, impoverished job-seekers, some who had seen better times but also some 'who had made it'; and all with varying aspirations, but united by the need to earn a living.

Subsequent generations have moved on, with an improved standard of living bearing no resemblance to that of their forebears. West Ham still attracts a diverse population from an even greater range of cultures but still with the unifying desire to find work and raise families. They too will move on, as we did.

Not everyone however has had, or will have the good fortune to take their 'street' with them. On a recent visit to the District Six Museum in Cape Town, I learnt that, after the streets were bulldozed in 1966 in the name of apartheid, the street signs were secretly salvaged and hidden in a cellar. I began to wonder what had happened to all the street signs of West Ham which had become obsolete when there were no streets in which to hang them and I was determined that Wharf Street, E16 would not finish up in the scrapyard. I am now delighted to report that I have received through the post a long rigid parcel measuring 4 feet by nine inches and covered with nineteen postage stamps.

It was the Wharf Street E16 name plate which became redundant when the Durham Arms underwent a face lift.

Wharf Street E16 now hangs proudly on my house wall in Winchester and will eventually be framed by variegated ivy. It pleases me that a street sign from one of the most deprived areas in England should be placed on the wall of a house in one of the most affluent..

41
LONDON, NORTH EASTERN RAILWAY

After the Great War my father became a porter on the LNER, Hertfordshire Railway. My earliest recollection is at age three staying with my maternal grandparents in a nearby village where they owned a sweet shop and shoe repair business. My grandfather would tell me that I could only have sugar bonbons, nothing else. But the local schoolmaster would fill my little tummy with glacé pineapple until I felt quite queasy. I'm sure he meant it kindly.

As I became older, in the school holidays I stayed with my paternal grandmother in another village. We could only afford to travel about like this because my father worked on the railway. Grandmother seemed so strong (she was 80 years old) and walked me once a week into Hertford to shop and have her glass of stout. Hertford was four miles away!

She had a lovely cottage and garden with a little stream near the door. In a field nearby there was a large oak tree with a swing hanging from one of the branches. Unfortunately I never did get to swing on it as there was always a great big bull staring at me across the fence.

Grandma's food was good but so filling. Solid rice pudding, sweet dumplings and blackbird pie which was quite tasty. They became tangled in the fruit nets and food was not to be wasted. There was no carpet on the stairs but the treads were snow-white from constant scrubbing, as was the outside loo which had plenty of newspaper squares to read. I loved it all, except for the bull.

By the time I was 12 years old my father was the only person left on the railway station. There had previously been sixteen. He was now booking office clerk, shunter, porter, etc. etc. and even delivered goods to local factories by horse and dray, all for the princely sum of £2 per week and no uniform as in the earlier years.

But there was happiness too. I spent many hours at the station, helping him (I hope). When we got tired we had a good meal in the porter's room by a roaring fire as coal was plentiful.

Memories are wonderful. Thank God we have them still.

OLD AGE
Frank Hooley

Walk steadily, not hurriedly
Talk genially not fretfully
Eat heartily not frugally
You still have time

Sleep peacefully not restlessly
Wake eagerly not peevishly
Dress stylishly not slovenly
You still have time

Write pleasantly not chidingly
Read avidly not sparingly
Sing lustily not drearily
You still have time

Love tenderly not jealously
Loathe fleetingly not bitterly
Laugh merrily not scornfully
You will have time

Go graciously not grudgingly
When its time

"SHE INSISTS ON SLEEPING WITH HER NOTES UNDER HER PILLOW, DOCTOR, SO NO ONE CAN ADD 'DO NOT RESUSCITATE'"